CANOEING
AND
KAYAKING

American Red Cross

ISBN: 0-86536-020-0
© 1981 by
The American National Red Cross

Preface

Nationally and locally the American Red Cross is governed by volunteers, most of its duties are performed by volunteers, and it is financed by voluntary contributions.

It is a goal of the American Red Cross to promote individual well-being, to save human lives, and to prevent or reduce human suffering. In accordance with this goal, Safety Services provides public courses of instruction in the areas of first aid, water safety, and boating safety. These courses aid individuals and families in improving their safety and increasing their self-reliance.

The purpose of this program is to educate and train individuals and families in the safe and skilled use of canoes and kayaks. Such education and training will result in a reduction of personal injury, property damage, and loss of life caused by the unsafe use of canoes and kayaks by uninformed and unskilled paddlers.

Acknowledgments

This text has been condensed from the American Red Cross *Canoeing* textbook, 1977 edition, supplemented with contributions by the members of the Red Cross Canoeing Advisory Committee.

Special acknowledgment and thanks are extended to Robert Jay Evans and Robert Anderson, authors of *Kayaking,* as well as to members of the Training Committee of the American Canoe Association, for their full support and assistance in the development of this text and instructional program.

Appreciation is also extended to the American Whitewater Affiliation for permission to quote excerpts from its Safety Code.

In addition, appreciation and thanks are proffered to the many volunteers of the American Canoe Association, and to American Red Cross volunteer and paid staff, whose advice and cooperation have contributed greatly to the preparation of this text.

Raymond P. Miller II, director of Small Craft Safety, and Donald R. Jarrell, assistant director of Small Craft Safety, were responsible for the development and writing of the text. Illustrations are by Richard Guy.

Contents

CANOEING AND KAYAKING

Chapter 1

An Introduction to the Sport of Paddling

As in many other sports activities, successful participation in canoeing and kayaking requires some prior knowledge. As a beginner, you will need to make some decisions about paddling that to a large extent will determine your involvement in the sport. It is often thought that it is difficult to achieve safety in a sport that has as many different aspects as paddling does, but that is not true. The one thing that all experienced paddlers can agree on is that safety in paddling is a matter of education. You should take advantage of the many organized classes in canoeing and kayaking before you venture onto the water. This education will lead to a greater understanding of paddling, which in turn will lead to a safer, more enjoyable contact with this dynamic sport.

This first chapter should provide enough information so that you may more wisely decide which craft to learn to paddle and which class to enroll in. It will also tell you about the requisite swimming skill and the proper use of a life jacket and will give you general information about how to care for your equipment—and yourself—under various circumstances. Part of the Introduction to Paddling session should be the opportunity to get into, get out of, capsize, balance, and rescue the craft you are interested in. These actions are most often performed in a pool session, which gives you the opportunity to touch, sit in, sit on, and in general get the feel of the boat you want to learn to paddle. Why learn to paddle a canoe when you may really want to paddle a kayak?

Search out pool sessions or other introductory programs in your community. The American Red Cross, the American Canoe Association (ACA) affiliate or club, or other local paddling organizations can help you find these programs.

Chapter I also deals with how to get into and out of various craft properly and how to exit safely from a boat when it is capsized. In addition, it describes elementary forms of rescue. A key aspect of safety is to be prepared for the things that may go wrong. Always be prepared to end up in the water.

Once you have finished this chapter and have participated in an actual Introduction to Paddling session, you will be ready to enroll in a fundamental paddling course that will teach you what you need to know about handling the boat of your choice.

There are several things to consider before you board a canoe or kayak to learn about its characteristics: such things as your swimming ability, your attire, and the equipment and its use. Let us examine each of these in turn.

SWIMMING ABILITY

Do you have to be able to swim before you learn to paddle? Some nonswimmers have learned to paddle well enough to become nationally recognized paddlers, but that is not generally the case. Often, a person who cannot swim has problems that are difficult to overcome. Among these is the fear of drowning, which is quite strong in almost all nonswimmers. This fear seriously impairs the nonswimmer's ability to learn to paddle. You will not be at ease *on* the water if you are not at ease *in* the water.

Another problem is one that is felt by your fellow paddlers. They must always be aware of your safety because when you capsize—and you are almost certainly going to—you may not have the swimming ability to effect a self-rescue. In other words, concern for you becomes a burden to the group.

How well must you be able to swim? Preferably, at least at the Red Cross Advanced Beginner level of proficiency. But if you can perform the following skills with ease, you have enough "water confidence" to enable you to survive any accidental immersion at this stage of your development.

1. Jump into deep water (6 feet or more) fully clothed and swim, tread water, float, bob, or otherwise stay afloat unaided for 5 minutes.

2. Properly put on an approved life jacket that is thrown to you while you are in deep water.

This self-check should be supervised by a good swimmer. Never swim alone.

ATTIRE
If you are about to experiment with these craft in the water, you must be dressed accordingly. At an indoor pool, or in a warm outside environment, a swim suit and sneakers will suffice. On warm sunny days outdoors, you may need protection from the sun and insects. In colder environments, however, you will need clothing that will keep you warm even when you are wet. A diver's wetsuit is best, but wool is better than most other materials. If you wear eyeglasses do not forget to use straps to hold them on. Sneakers help protect your feet from possible roughness in the boat and in walking about on shore. When paddling in kayaks and other decked boats, some people prefer to wear long pants to protect their legs from possible rough spots inside the boat.

Hypothermia
Without the proper attire, you increase your risk of suffering from hypothermia. This condition is a

reduction in the temperature of the body, often caused by cold, wet, and windy weather or by immersion in cold water. A person suffering from hypothermia gradually loses physical coordination, and his thinking becomes cloudy—not a good situation for someone in an isolated locale who has only himself to rely on for his well-being. Because of the constant threat of hypothermia around the water, proper attire is essential.

EQUIPMENT

Life Jackets

A life jacket—or personal flotation device (PFD)—is undoubtedly the most important piece of equipment you will own. It serves three purposes. First, and perhaps most important, it is designed to keep you at the surface of the water (or buoy you up). Second, it can provide a certain amount of protection against injury to your back and lower spine (especially valuable in river paddling). And third, if properly designed and fitted, it can reduce heat loss from the body, which helps in preventing

the onset of hypothermia when you are in cold water. Approved U.S. Coast Guard life jackets fall into five categories, Types I through V. For our purposes, two types—II and III—are most satisfactory for paddling. Most Type I devices are too bulky, and the Type IV is not "a wearable." Although the Type V device is not generally acceptable for recreational boating, some devices of this kind are satisfactory.

Type II

The Type II life jacket (Fig. 1–1A) is suitable for flat-water canoeing. As you see, it offers no protection to the back and only minimal thermal protection. These two factors—and your keen sense of safety—reduce its use in river canoeing or in any form of kayaking. Its bulk also makes it unsuitable for these activities.

Type III

Some Type III life jackets (Fig. 1–1B) are designed specifically for the paddler. Called a special purpose device, the Type III is built to offer

Fig. 1–1A

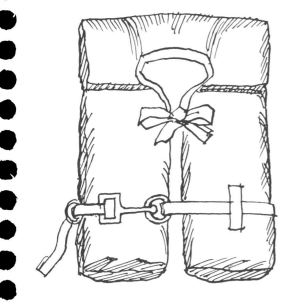

Fig. 1–1B

Common style of Type II device designed to turn the wearer, in the water, to a vertical or slightly backward position. Has at least 15.5 pounds of buoyancy.

Common style of Type III devices designed to maintain the wearer, in the water, in a vertical or slightly backward position. Has at least 15.5 pounds of buoyancy.

the buoyancy and protection the paddler needs and at the same time to provide greater freedom of movement. These Type III devices should offer protection to the back and lower spine.

Life Jacket Selection

When selecting a life jacket, keep in mind your ultimate goals as a paddler. If one of these goals is that you want to be an occasional flat-water voyageur, then a Type II may serve you well. But if you aspire to become a frequent paddler, by all means purchase a good Type III that is made to your specifications. Your instructor can help you in this regard. Before you decide to buy, you should try your life jacket in the water to insure proper fit and comfort, both in and out of the water.

Wearing a Life Jacket

A properly fitted life jacket should feel only slightly constricting. This feeling indicates a firm fit. Even then, you may want to fit your life jacket with a crotch strap. Loose life jackets will ride up on you when you are in the water, impairing your vision and your movements.

It is prudent to wear your life jacket at all times while you are paddling. By doing so you are prepared for nearly any eventuality. For instance, you are ready to enter the water either intentionally or as a result of capsizing. It is important to keep the life jacket zipped up or tied securely while you are wearing it, thus avoiding the possibility of its coming off at an inopportune moment. With the Type II yoke design it is most important to keep the neck-tie tied at all times. At no time is a life jacket to be knelt upon or used as a cushion. This improper use will quickly destroy the device.

Once you get a life jacket of your own, or one that fits and that you will be borrowing for a period of time, put it on and get into the water. This "test" will give you the extra confidence of knowing that the life jacket will buoy you up. The test will also give you a chance to work on moving about and swimming with a life jacket on. In addition, it will help identify the peculiarities of the specific life jacket that could cause you problems in an emergency situation. (As with the swim test, you should enter the water only with adequate supervision.)

Boats and Paddles

Canoes and kayaks are the subject at hand. You should know enough about them to be able to say, "That is a C-1," or, "That is a kayak." C-1? Kayak? Open canoe? All are quite different (Fig. 1–2).

The traditional, or Canadian, canoe is what is commonly termed an open canoe. It may be built of wood, aluminum, plastic, or some combination of all three. Figure 1–3 shows a typical open canoe that could be built from any of the materials mentioned. The basic nomenclature of the canoe is applicable to all open canoes regardless of construction materials. Even then only a few of the more technical names differ.

The kayak shown in Figure 1–4, with appropriate basic nomenclature, is a typical slalom kayak and is quite different from the open canoe. The

Fig. 1–2
Typical canoes and kayaks

Slalom kayak (K-1)

Slalom canoe (C-1)

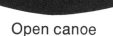

Open canoe

Slalom canoe (C-2)

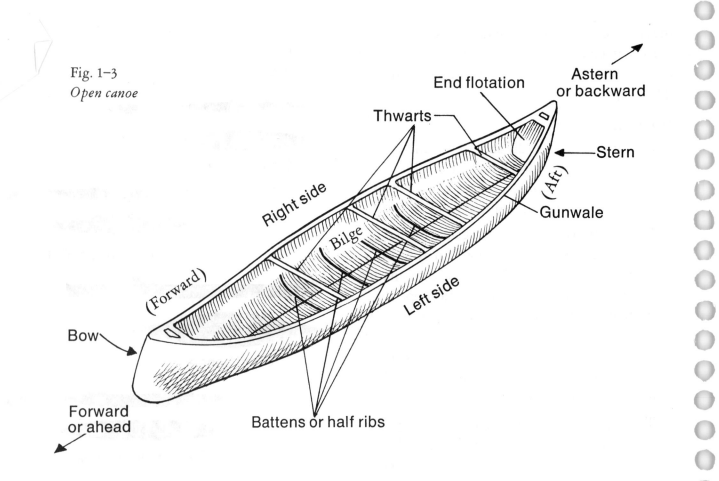

Fig. 1–3
Open canoe

End flotation

Astern
or backward

Thwarts

Stern

Right side

(Aft)

Bilge

Gunwale

(Forward)

Left side

Bow

Battens or half ribs

Forward
or ahead

1.8

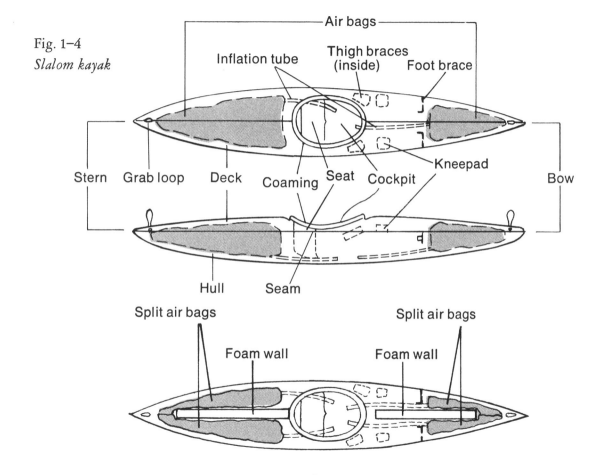

Fig. 1–4
Slalom kayak

Air bags

Inflation tube

Thigh braces (inside)

Foot brace

Stern   Grab loop   Deck   Coaming   Seat   Cockpit   Kneepad   Bow

Hull   Seam

Split air bags   Split air bags

Foam wall   Foam wall

1.9

kayak is often referred to as a decked, or closed, boat because the interior of the craft is enclosed except for an opening (cockpit) for the paddler. To make this opening watertight, the paddler wears a spray skirt that attaches to the coaming around the cockpit. This kayak is referred to as a K-1, indicating a kayak for one person.

In addition to slalom kayaks there are also touring kayaks, some of which are K-2's (Fig. 1–5). These types are primarily for touring and flat-water paddling. The K-2 (decked kayak) is not often found on rivers, nor has it proven to be suitable for any but the mildest moving water except in the hands of expert paddlers. There are both advantages and disadvantages to paddling either a canoe or a kayak. First of all, because the open canoe has no decking to speak of, you may paddle from several different positions. This choice of position enables you to properly trim the craft (or level it in the water) for a variety of circumstances: traveling in wind, with equipment, or with another paddler. Also, the canoe can be equipped with sail or motor or can be poled. As a result, the canoeist has a greater choice of activities than does the K-1 paddler or the touring kayaker (Fig. 1–6).

The K-1, however, is more maneuverable than an open canoe. Your center of gravity is lower, which aids in stability, and you propel the kayak with a double-bladed paddle. In addition, with the paddler enclosed in the kayak from the waist down by a spray skirt that keeps water out of the craft, the kayak can be handled in quite turbulent water.

Both the canoe and the kayak are generally accepted for activities such as touring, camping, fishing, and river running. Both are heavily involved in regional, national, and international competitions.

There are other craft afloat that you should be aware of, but they are beyond the intended scope of this text. Therefore, only a brief mention here is called for.

The C-1 and C-2 (decked boats) are examples of these other craft. Although the C-1 is much like the K-1 in looks, it differs in use and also differs

Fig. 1–5
A touring K-2

Fig. 1–6

Canoes can be used in a variety of activities, such as motoring, poling, or sailing.

slightly in dimensions. Generally, a C-1 is wider and deeper than a K-1 and is paddled from the kneeling position rather than from a seated one as in the kayak. All canoes (C-1, C-2, and open boats) are propelled with a single-bladed paddle, whereas the kayak is propelled with a double-bladed paddle.

The selection of a proper-sized paddle in the beginning stages of learning to paddle is not crucial. Generally speaking, a modern design canoe paddle that when set upright on its tip comes to about eye level or nose level, should be suitable. Kayak paddles should be from 6½ to 7 feet in length with offset blades, that is, blades that are set at 90-degree angles to each other. More specific guidelines are found in Chapters 3 and 4.

USE OF BOATS
Carrying and Launching

Sooner or later you are going to have to pick up and move or launch a canoe or a kayak. Carrying and launching these lightweight craft is not difficult, nor does it take a great deal of finesse, although there are better methods than dragging and dropping.

First of all, you must remember to lift with your legs, to prevent back injury, not your arms and back. Second, even though today's boats are far from delicate, you must treat them as if they were. Observing these rules will preserve both you and the boat, so that you may paddle still another day.

A few methods of carrying and launching are shown in Figures 1–7 through 1–13. As you can see, more hands make the work seem easier.

Getting Into Canoes and Kayaks

The subject we are considering here is paddling positions and balance. Remember that whenever you are working with canoes or kayaks on the water you should wear a properly fitted life jacket. Wearing such a device affords good protection and helps to establish a good habit, the importance of which cannot be too strongly stressed.

Fig. 1–7

Two-person carry. Grip should be secure and comfortable.

Fig. 1–8

Two-person, on-the-shoulder carry

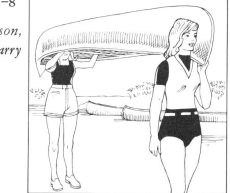

◁ Fig. 1–9
Four-person carry is used for heavy canoes or by smaller people.

Fig. 1–10 ▷
Two-person canoe launching

◁ Fig. 1–11
One-person, on-the-shoulder kayak carry

Fig. 1–12 ▷
Two-person kayak carry using grab loops

1.14

Fig. 1–13

Kayak launching

For your Introduction to Paddling session, you should be at a swimming pool or a beach, with a qualified instructor. What you should do in an Introduction to Paddling session is discussed below.

The Canoe

You can quickly and easily master getting into and out of a canoe without getting wet (Fig. 1–14) if you remember the following important points:

- Keep your center of gravity low and move slowly and deliberately.

- Transfer your weight slowly from shore to the bottom center of the canoe.

- Board your canoe directly into your paddling position whenever possible.

- For maximum control and stability always kneel in canoes, even though some canoes have seats.

- Equipment should already be aboard in a convenient location when you get into the canoe.

To get out of the canoe, simply reverse the steps described above.

Fig. 1–14
Boarding canoe at dockside

The bow and stern paddlers should not exchange positions while they are in the canoe. It is usually easier and certainly safer to go to shore, exit from the canoe, and re-enter in the desired positions.

The Kayak

Before launching your kayak, you should make sure that the boat "fits" you. A kayak is literally worn and must be properly fitted so that you can use it effectively. Use the procedures described below to enter the kayak while you and the boat are still on shore (on soft ground or grass) and adjust the boat to fit you. You should fit firmly in the seat and not be able to slide from side to side or back and forth. Your knees or thighs should brace against the pads as your feet press gently on the foot braces. Most kayaks have adjustable foot braces. The seat may be shimmed with some foam plastic and tape to provide a firmer fit. Be sure that you can also exit easily from the boat.

Getting into and out of a kayak, with its tiny, restricted cockpit, poses a little more of a challenge than does getting into and out of a canoe.

To get into a kayak, place it in the water parallel to shore. Squat down next to the cockpit, on land, facing the bow. Rest the paddle across the kayak, just behind the cockpit, with one of the blades lying flat on the ground for support. With the hand nearest the boat, grip the paddle shaft and the rear of the cockpit (thumb toward the stern). This keeps the boat surprisingly steady. Grasp the shaft with the other hand (Fig. 1–15A). Support

Fig. 1–15A
Boarding a kayak. Use the paddle to steady the kayak and support your weight.

your weight with your arms while you first place one leg then the other into the kayak. Shifting your body weight last, lower yourself into the seat, straightening your legs as you do (Fig. 1–15B).

Fig. 1–15B
Extend your legs into the kayak before sitting in the seat.

If you do not straighten your legs as you slip into the seat, your torso and knees will extend out of the kayak, and you will be unable to get your legs into the boat unless you back out and start again. To get out, reverse the procedures described above.

NOTE. While practicing with canoes and kayaks, wear your life jacket, helmet, shoes (tennis shoes), and swimsuit.

Canoe and Kayak Stability

Once aboard your canoe or kayak, you will soon find how stable these craft can be. A well-fitted kayak should respond to your every move. The kayak is controlled not only with paddle strokes but also with body movements.

You will undoubtedly try the limits of stability by rocking the boat while shifting your weight from side to side. If you have not done so, you should. While keeping your weight over the center line of the boat, forceably tip the boat as far as you can, using your hips. Do this to both sides repeatedly. Isn't it amazing just how stable these so-called tippy boats are? But if you lean your body out over the water, you will get wet. You are now ready to learn the emergency procedures connected with capsizing.

The Wet Exit

This maneuver is the one way of getting out of your canoe or kayak that you hope you will seldom use. You will practice it over and over under controlled circumstances until it becomes second nature to you, so that you can feel secure in knowing that you will not be trapped upside down in your boat in a real capsizing situation away from controlled practice. Being caught or trapped in the boat is a serious concern of novice paddlers.

Canoe Capsizing

One concern in canoe capsizing is that of being struck on the head by the canoe during the capsizing. Knowing where you are in relation to the canoe will do much to avoid this hazard; keep your eyes open.

Once you have capsized, relax and make contact with the canoe with your hands if you have not already done so. Stay upside down long enough to extract your feet and legs from the

canoe, then surface, *maintaining contact with the canoe;* keep your eyes open.

If you had a partner when you capsized, you should still have one. Check to be sure.

You will discover that nearly all canoes (except those constructed of wood or ABS* plastic) will float upright. Permit the canoe to do so and swim it to shore. You will also find that wearing your life jacket really helps. Once at shore you can empty the water from the canoe (Figs.1–16A, B, C).

Fig. 1–16A

Emptying water from a canoe. Once the water is out, set the canoe down, turn it over, and it is ready to launch again.

---

*ABS is the abbreviation for acrylonitrile-butadiene-styrene, a modern thermoplastic that usually consists of a series of layers, including a foam core that makes the material buoyant.

Fig. 1–16B

Fig. 1–16C

Kayak Capsizing

For the kayak, the wet exit must be practiced over and over again. You must be at ease and not in any way apprehensive about capsizing in a kayak. It is easy to get out of a kayak *if you do it slowly and deliberately*. Your instructor should first have you practice this skill without the spray skirt (Figs. 1–17A, B, C, D).

Fig. 1–17A

Wet exit from a kayak (shown from under water). Release spray skirt from the cockpit, then somersault out. Maintain contact with the kayak at all times.

Fig. 1–17B

Fig. 1–17C

Fig. 1–17D

In shallow lake or pool water (3 to 4 feet deep), with supervision and safety nearby, purposely capsize the kayak; tip it over while you are properly seated in it. Then, release the spray skirt from the coaming and take your feet off the foot braces. Carefully bend forward toward the deck and push yourself out of the kayak, using your hands on the cockpit coaming. Slowly extract your legs and feet until you are free. It is especially important to wear a helmet while you practice in shallow water or where the water is cloudy and the bottom uneven.

Once out of the kayak, swim to one end, grab the grab loop, and swim with the boat to shore or the side of the pool. You will notice that the kayak is upside down. *Leave it that way.* The trapped air prevents more water from entering and keeps the boat light and easy to move.

Inflated flotation bags or inner tubes are a boon to all craft. They displace water (which makes the boat lighter when swamped) and facilitate emptying the capsized boat. Emptying is a relatively easy procedure with a canoe—but most difficult with a kayak until the knack is perfected.

Emptying the kayak involves holding the boat upside down and alternately raising and lowering one end so that the water will run out of the cockpit. It is possible to do this alone or with assistance (Figs. 1–18A, B, C).

Fig. 1–18A

Emptying water from a kayak, using the shore to support one end

Fig. 1–18B

On shore, empty water by rocking the upside-down kayak on your thigh.

Fig. 1–18C

Rescue

At some point in your efforts to acquaint yourself with canoes and kayaks you will end up in the water. In the pool, or other supervised setting, that is not likely to be a problem. But as you become more experienced in the use of your craft, you may unexpectedly swim in more hostile settings. You must know how to cope with these situations.

After a wet exit, the simplest form of self-rescue is to hold on to the craft and hand paddle it to shore, or even to re-enter the craft and swim it to shore. But if the safety of shore is off in the distance or if the water is cold, other techniques are needed. Techniques such as the Capistrano flip, canoe-over-canoe, kayak-over-kayak, the Eskimo roll, and throwing ropes are likely to be demonstrated to you in your introduction to paddling, but your best opportunity to learn these rescue techniques is in a formal course of instruction.

Rescue techniques consist of both self-rescue (how to take care of yourself in an emergency) and rescue of others. The latter come in two basic forms. First, those that assist others to reach shore, either by your reaching out from shore (using a throw rope) or by your towing them with your boat. Second, those that by your assistance get people out of the water, either back into their own craft or aboard yours. The first set of techniques is perfectly fine whenever shore or safety is close at hand, but on open water where shore or safety is far away, the second set is more appropriate.

Remember, never enter the water yourself to rescue people or equipment unless there is absolutely no other way. Even then, you must give careful consideration to circumstances and your own ability.

CONCLUSIONS

We have now taken you through the essential elements of a typical Introduction to Paddling session. All the information in this section should be brought to your attention and taught by your instructor.

Many introductory sessions end with a paddling demonstration by one of the local experts and with films. Schedules of organized classes, from basic kayaking through canoe poling and sailing, are usually made public at this time. These classes are often taught by excellent volunteer instructors. You may, however, be asked to pay a nominal

rental fee for the use of equipment, which is only fair.

Many excellent commercial courses in paddling are also available. The staff of commercial classes are often top paddlers who are also skilled teachers.

As you can see, there are many ways to get into paddling. Take advantage of the courses available to you. You will learn more in a shorter period of time and be able to get on the water right away, with a keen sense of safe paddling. Such preparation leads to complete enjoyment of the sport.

As you progress as a paddler, you will need both to learn more and to perfect what you already know. One of the best ways to do so is to associate with better paddlers by joining an organized club that prides itself on its safety record.

If you are in an area with none of the foregoing choices available, you must search out those people in your vicinity that have experience and an apparently safe attitude about paddling. With these people to help you, and this manual, you can progress safely toward your goals as a paddler. By all means, do not blunder onto water for which you are not prepared. Take each step cautiously and deliberately, calculating both the risks and the limits of your knowledge and ability.

Chapter 2
Fundamentals of Paddling

Once you know the type of craft you wish to learn to paddle, it is time to enroll in a specific course. The courses in the fundamentals of paddling will help you to master your craft in a calm water environment. They will cover everything necessary for you to enjoy an outing from home, onto the water, and back again safely. It makes no difference whether you choose the canoe or the kayak to paddle, since many of the fundamentals are common to both types of craft. This chapter will cover these fundamentals: planning a trip, ropework, transporting your craft, emergency repairs, and care of equipment.

PLANNING A TRIP

Included in the preparation of an enjoyable and successful trip are the following:

- Selection of your travel companions
- Selection of locale and route
- Selection of necessary equipment
- Food and cooking gear

- Selection of a leader
- Preparation for possible emergencies

Traveling Companions

Choose your party carefully. This factor is important whether you are organizing a trip or joining someone else's trip. You must be able to get along with the group, for a number of reasons. Among these is the matter of safety. Total cooperation is needed should an emergency situation arise. Such cooperation is difficult at best if one or two of the group are not in agreement or are dissatisfied for some reason.

Sharing the workload, having the same goals for the trip, and having enough skill and stamina to keep up with the party are other examples of getting along with your companions. The longer the trip, the more important these considerations become.

Locale and Route

The entire group should agree upon the location and duration of the trip and on how difficult the trip should be. The leader must be sure to keep the trip within the capabilities of the group. However, should you be joining a trip that has already been organized, you must be honest with yourself and the group as to your abilities. In other words, know the limits of your ability as well as those of the group members. If it seems that anyone in the group has overextended his ability, or that the trip is beyond your ability, this may not be the trip for you.

Detailed planning enhances the level of safety for your trip. Some of the best information is available in guidebooks written specifically for canoeists. These books will indicate possible campsites, river hazards, and portage trails. Printed information, including maps, is often available through local, state, or federal agencies. When your plans have been completed, let others know the details: specifically, who is in the group, where you are going, and when you plan to return. In some popular canoeing areas it is necessary to apply or register in advance and to sign in and out of the area.

Necessary Equipment

In making up an equipment list, try to include everything that you think is necessary for the enjoyment of your trip. Then shorten the list considerably by eliminating those items that are not absolutely necessary. Take only equipment that is in good shape.

The duration of the trip (in hours or even days) and the length of possible portages will inevitably dictate the amount of equipment to be taken. A good motto here is, When in doubt, leave it out.

A simple list would include:

- Ground sheet
- Sleeping bag
- First aid kit
- Rope
- Flashlight
- Air mattress or foam pad
- Tent or other shelter
- Extra clothes
- Toilet kit
- Fire kit
- Waterproof packs
- Water bottles

A book on camping is your best source of specific information regarding the type and amount of gear necessary for a camping trip. In canoe camping you can take more weight and bulk than a backpacker can but less than you can in car camping.

Consulting with your trip leader and other more experienced paddlers in your group will aid you greatly in selecting the right equipment.

Food and Cooking Gear

As with equipment, you must take into account the length of the trip and its relation to the weight factor of food and cooking gear. The question is not what you can use but what you can do without.

One-day or overnight trips are easy to plan for. Since the time involved is of short duration, a certain amount of sacrifice can be tolerated: extra items can be carried, less food can be consumed, or less appetizing food can be served.

Those trips of longer duration, however, require more appetizing and more nourishing meals. The following suggestions will be helpful to you in understanding what is necessary on three-, four-, or five-day trips. The longer the trip, the more important the menus.

- The food must be of minimum weight yet must have adequate food value.
- The food should be readily digestible and balanced among fat, protein, and carbohydrate.
- The food must have good keeping qualities and must be packaged conveniently.
- It must be easy to prepare the food quickly, with simple equipment.
- Salt (because of loss during strenuous activity) should be part of your dietary intake. Salt your food.
- Think about drinking water, it is a must. If it is not available on the trip it must be taken along.

Selection of a Leader

For a leader the group should agree on a person who has spent considerable time paddling in the kind of area the group will venture into and who has had some training as a leader. Do not base the selection of a leader on paddling ability only.

Formal leadership is really not what you are after. The person selected should be able to guide the group in all phases of the trip and take charge when a crisis arises. This ability requires experience, maturity, judgment, and knowledge. A good leader considers the well-being of all the members of the group. Whatever form leadership takes, the group should respect it—and the leader should, in turn, respect the members of the group. Above all, *do not attempt a trip on any lake, stream, or river without competent leadership.*

Preparation for Possible Emergencies

The most important element in your preparation for possible emergencies is first aid training. Such training should include cardiopulmonary resuscitation (CPR) and an understanding of hypothermia. You should not set out on any trip without having someone in the group who is trained in, and experienced in giving, first aid.

Life jackets should be worn at all times while you are on rough water. Also, each person in the group should swim well enough so as not to constitute a hazard to himself or others.

Everyone in the party should have the ability to rescue personnel and equipment in case of capsizing. It is wise to have a session in rescue procedures just before your trip, and your trip leader should know how to reach emergency assistance along your route.

Be sure to file a "float plan" with a neighbor or a relative, telling them where you are going, how long you expect to be gone, and who is going with you.

Check the weather just before your trip. Safe travel requires at least moderately good weather.

Above all, be prepared.

The primary consideration facing you if you intend to paddle in the wilderness or down a river for any length of time is that of your own limitations. Knowledge of these limitations, coupled with a knowledge of the hazards you are likely to confront, will do much toward making your trip a success.

If you have difficulty in realistically determining these factors, get in touch with an experienced trip leader who can help you with such an assessment. It is important that you trust the judgment of the trip leader.

ROPEWORK

Once you have made your plans regarding who is going and where you are going and for how long, the time has come to load the equipment and go. To transport your equipment, you need to know how to secure it for travel, which will involve the use of ropes and knots. Rope (line) is useful in numerous instances: tying articles on cartops, portaging, launching, rescuing, and many other activities. Therefore, it is necessary to learn enough about ropes and knots to use safe methods of tying or securing when these are needed.

Varieties and Uses of Rope

Rope is made of a variety of materials and in a multitude of sizes. Each kind has its good and bad points. Different materials vary in strength. The newer, synthetic ropes are smaller and lighter than natural fiber ropes of the same strength, offering an obvious advantage. However, a small-diameter rope may be too small for comfortable, or even safe, handling in stress situations.

The cost of rope varies with its material, size, and tensile strength. This cost plays an important role in the selection of the rope to be used. Many people try to get by with less expensive rope when good quality is needed.

The following information covers the general care required for any kind of rope:

- When it is not in use, keep rope coiled neatly in a dry, cool place, out of direct sunlight.

- Keep rope as clean as possible. It can be damaged from within by grit and dirt that have found their way into the braid or weave. When tension is applied, the grit inside will cut fibers, thus weakening the rope.

- Replace damaged or worn rope. If ropes are needed in an emergency and they are not in good condition, the problem at hand could be made much worse.

- Avoid stepping on rope, since that damages it and shortens its useful life.

- Make sure that all rope used is finished off on the ends, so that it will not fray or unlay. Synthetic rope can be melted to produce a smooth, neat, secure end that is not larger than the rest of the rope. Whipping the ends will finish off other kinds of rope.

Ropes of synthetic fiber have virtually replaced those of natural fiber on and around the water because of their greater strength and durability. Twisted natural-fiber ropes should be whipped and dipped in a lasting coating to protect the whipping. Whipping can be accomplished by the use of flax or cotton twine (Fig. 2-1).

The twine should be treated with a mixture of beeswax and resin to strengthen and waterproof it. (A waterproof adhesive tape can be used as a temporary whipping for any rope.)

Rope is of either a laid or a braided construction. There is a diamond braid, commonly found in construction of polypropylene ropes, and a solid braid, more commonly used with nylon or Dacron. A solid braid is more convenient, as it is less likely to kink and is easier to use (Fig. 2–2).

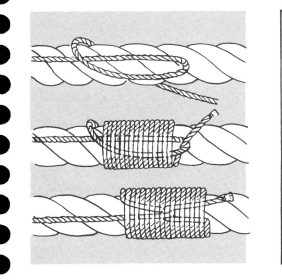

Fig. 2–1
Whipping the end of a line. The end should be whipped before the rope is cut.

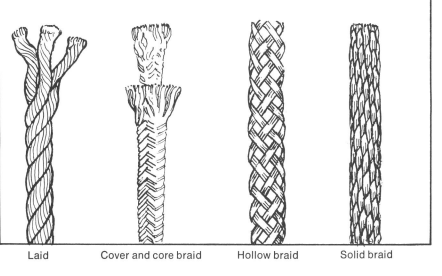

| Laid | Cover and core braid | Hollow braid | Solid braid |

Fig. 2–2
Modern rope construction

Specific uses for different types of ropes for paddling activities are recommended below.

- Polypropylene, from ⅜ to ½ inch in diameter, is recommended for use as a rescue rope because of its light weight, low elasticity, and floatability. However, it is slippery and does not hold knots well. Any rope used for rescue purposes should not be used for anything else, since its strength should be preserved for lifesaving.

- Nylon is used universally in paddling. It will outlast most other rope and is very elastic and strong but does not float. It can be used for anchor lines, mooring ropes, rescue lines, and end lines. It can also be used for tie-downs, but you must be careful because of the elasticity of nylon.

- Dacron is very similar to nylon except that it is not as elastic. Its uses are the same as those for nylon, especially where stretching under tension is undesirable.

Knots, Bends, and Hitches

Your safety and that of your equipment depend on your knowledge of the use of rope. This knowledge includes the proper application of a few simple knots, bends, and hitches, which will fit your needs in nearly every aspect of paddling where a tie is needed.

Knots

Knots are generally used in binding objects together or in forming a temporary loop in a rope.

- The *square knot,* or *reef knot,* is probably the most widely known of all knots. Its only use around kayaks and canoes, however, is for lashing items to the craft or for tying gear together (Fig. 2–3).

- The *bowline* (Fig. 2–4) is perhaps the most useful and reliable knot that can be used around boats. It is used to put a loop into the end of a rope; such a loop can be used in a multitude of ways.

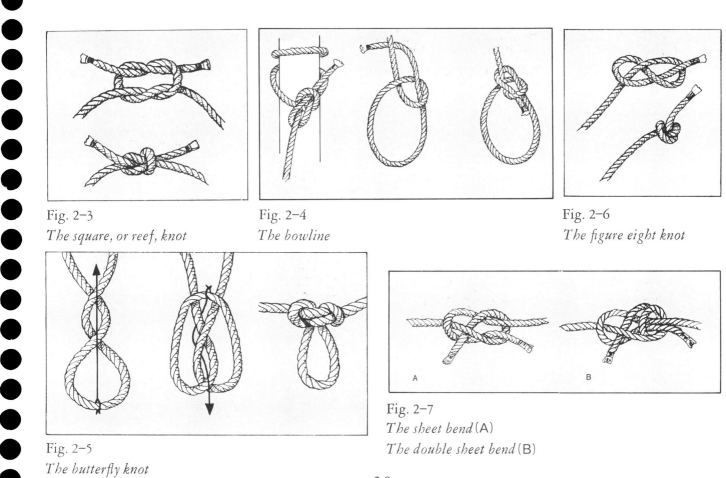

Fig. 2–3
The square, or reef, knot

Fig. 2–4
The bowline

Fig. 2–6
The figure eight knot

Fig. 2–5
The butterfly knot

Fig. 2–7
The sheet bend(A)
The double sheet bend(B)

2.9

- The *butterfly knot* (Fig. 2–5) is most useful in forming an eye in the middle of a rope. It does not easily jam and it provides something to grab onto when the fingers are cold and numb.
- The *figure eight knot* (Fig. 2–6) makes a stopper to keep the end of a rope from running through a confined opening. It can also be used at the end of a throw rope. The figure eight knot is easily untied and it will not jam.

Bends

Bends are used in joining two ropes together.
- The *sheet bend* (Fig. 2–7) is excellent for tying two ropes together, especially two ropes of unequal diameter. It is trustworthy and easily understood. An additional turn can be taken to make a double sheet bend, which is even more secure.
- The *Englishman's bend,* or *fisherman's knot,* is another bend used to tied two ropes together (Fig. 2–8). It is made by tying two overhand knots back to back with their ends pointing in opposite directions. Once tight, this knot is nearly impossible to untie, especially if the ropes were wet when tension was applied.
- The *Rosendahl bend,* or *Zeppelin knot* (Fig. 2–9), will not jam under heavy loads, as may the sheet bend, the bowline, or the Englishman's bend. It distributes the load evenly throughout the knot and can always be quickly untied. It can only be used with ropes of equal size.

Hitches

Hitches are used to secure a rope to another object.
- The *clove hitch* (Fig. 2–10) is a simple tie that can be used in various circumstances. It is quick to tie and easy to remember.
- The *rolling hitch* (Fig. (2-12) is a more dependable knot than the clove hitch and is more often used when a line is being attached to a smooth surface or to a larger rope. The pull can be parallel with the item tied to, or perpendicular to it.
- The *tautline, or midshipman's, hitch* (Fig. 2-13) , is so called because it can be used to take up slack in a rope or to exert a small

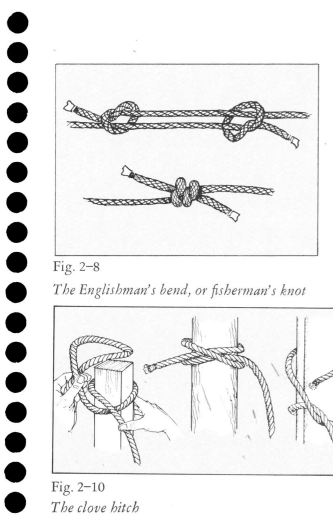

Fig. 2–8

The Englishman's bend, or fisherman's knot

Fig. 2–10

The clove hitch

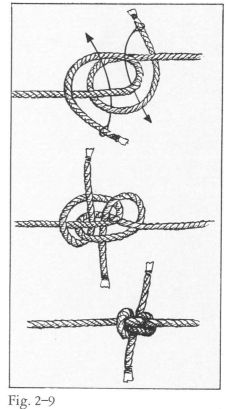

Fig. 2–9

The Rosendahl bend, or Zeppelin knot

Two half hitches
Fig. 2–11

2.11

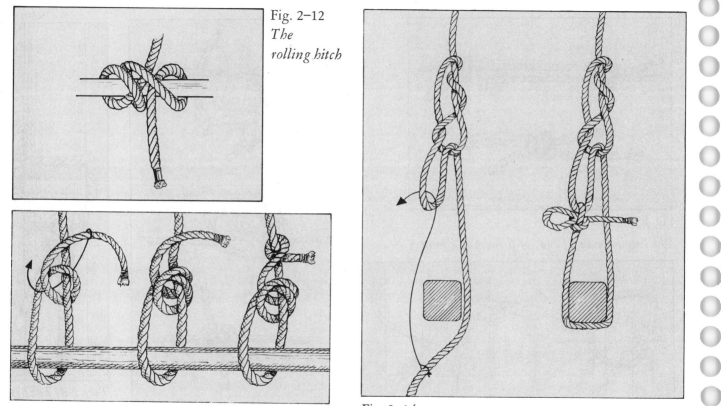

Fig. 2–12
*The
rolling hitch*

Fig. 2–13
The tautline, or midshipman's, hitch

Fig. 2–14
*The diver's hitch, finished with a slipped
half hitch*

amount of strain between two objects. This hitch is useful for tying the ends of boats to car bumpers.

- The *diver's hitch* (Fig. 2-14) is extremely useful when two objects must be tied very tightly together, for example, when a boat is tied to a trailer or to roof racks. This hitch does not jam. Form a bight in the rope coming from one object by taking two twists in the rope. Bring a bight from the running end through the aforementioned bight. Pass the running end around or through the other object and back through the second bight. This can be done a second time, thus increasing the leverage. Excessive force, however, will damage the rope. Tie off as shown.

Armed with a working knowledge of rope and knots, you are prepared to load the boats and equipment and to start your trip.

TRANSPORTING YOUR CRAFT

This subject is one of the most important to be discussed. The responsibility for moving your boat —whether it is borrowed, rented, or owned—from the livery or your residence to the water is yours. Such responsibility is many-faceted. It ranges from an inspection of the vehicle's capacity for carrying your boat, to a knowledge of the state laws regarding the moving by vehicle of items such as your boat.

Many trips have been cut short or totally ruined because boats have been damaged when they were improperly secured to trailers or roof racks. Other trips have begun or ended on a sour note when state police issued citations because of the improper carrying of boats or equipment. It is therefore important that you understand this section on cartop carrying of canoes and kayaks.

Cartop Carrying

There are two important factors to consider before you secure boats to a cartop carrier: the reliability of the carrier and the reliability of the ropes or other tie-downs.

The material used to tied down boats to racks and bumpers should be of sufficient quality and strength to withstand the abuse it is subjected to. Nylon rope with a minimum diameter of ¼ inch is recommended. In general, rope is far superior to straps, which are supplied with some carriers, and to elastic shock cord.

Shock cord is quick and efficient for securing boats to roof racks but is not suitable for end ties to bumpers. It is safest to use good quality rope all the way around.

The most reliable cartop carriers available are those designed to clamp securely to the car's rain gutters (Fig. 2-15) . The other varieties, such as suction cups and straps or turnbuckles, are not as reliable and should not be used for any long or rough drives.

The cross bars must be securely bolted to the clamp units and should show no signs of fatigue. Also, in many states, to be legal the cross bars should not extend beyond the sides of the automobile. If in doubt, ask your local police department

Fig. 2–15

Typical roof racks. Note the attachment to the rain gutters.

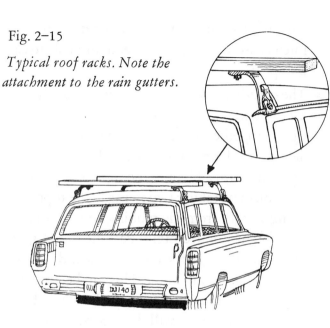

or state department of motor vehicles.

Carriers can be constructed with stops, uprights, or cradles for carrying specific boats. Several possibilities are shown in Figures 2–16A, B, C.

Carrying open boats on cartops can present some problems. For instance, how many boats can be

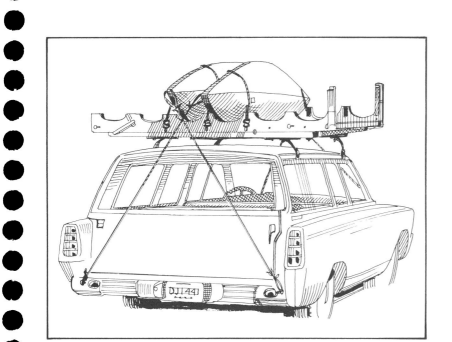

Fig. 2-16A

Two kayaks on edge. Note the contoured cradles on the cross bars.

Fig. 2-16B

A canoe and kayak properly secured. Note the crossing of the ropes at the ends of the boats, and the upright bar to lean the kayak against.

Fig. 2-16C

Boats should be centered over the vehicle to minimize the risk of their shifting forward or backward.

carried safely? Many auto makers specify a safe roofload weight in the owner's manual. Regardless of the number of boats being carried, each one should be securely tied to the racks. The diver's hitch is useful here, as is the clove hitch or even two half hitches.

Decked boats pose different problems. Because of their light construction, decked boats cannot be tied as tightly as open boats. The light deck is easily crushed if the boat is tied upside down. The usually stiffer hull is less subject to damage if the boat is secured right side up. But this method can result in distortion of the hull, which would adversely affect performance. This distortion problem can be minimized if a contoured and padded cradle is attached to the racks. Generally, the best way to carry decked boats on roof racks is to stack them on their sides on prepared racks. The boats, in addition to being secured to the roof racks, should have each end of each boat tied to the front and rear of the vehicle—usually from the grab loops to the bumpers.

When tying rope around bumpers, be careful not to tie around any sharp edges. If that is unavoidable, pad the rope. This problem can be avoided by the installation of adequately sized eye bolts in the bumpers. Such bolts not only protect the rope but facilitate tying.

Note that the boats on the outside of the racks (Figs. 2–16A, 16B) are secured in a specific way. The boat on the right side of the racks is secured to the left side of the car. The boat on the left, to the right. The boat in the center is secured to the outside boats. Boats on top of a group of boats must be secured separately to the bumpers.

The general principle for end ties is that the boats should be secured so that they are pulled toward the center and downward. Downward to help hold them onto the racks and toward the center to prevent the ends from shifting apart. End ties also serve to prevent the boats from sliding forward or backward. Check the tightness of all ties at each rest stop, especially if the equipment has been tied on overnight.

EMERGENCY REPAIRS

Emergency repairs are those that take place during a trip and that utilize materials at hand. Because it is not practical to carry the tools and materials for every contingency, repairs are usually of a temporary nature, although some may turn out to be permanent. The contents of your repair kit will depend on the construction of your craft and the length of the trip. The farther you travel from civilization, the more extensive the capabilities of your kit must be. On short trips a small roll of duct tape will suffice as your repair kit.

The most common type of emergency repair, regardless of the material your boat is made of, is stopping a leak. The leak may be due to a crack, puncture, tear, or other minor damage to the hull, and can easily be "field-repaired" if you use duct tape on the outside of the hull over the damaged area. Duct tape is readily available in 3-inch widths at any hardware store. Make sure the surface to be taped is clean, dry, and warm. Wipe the area clean and dry with a cloth and allow the sun

or a warm fire to further dry and warm the spot to be patched. Then place the tape over the damaged area and press smooth. Use overlapping strips of tape if necessary. Very large holes have been temporarily patched in this manner.

Duct tape is likely to be your single most effective repair material; you should have some with you on every trip. This tape alone is usually an adequate repair kit for any short trip. Two or three 3-foot lengths can be wound around your paddle shaft—a good storage idea, since duct tape is unaffected by water.

On more extended trips, additional repair materials may be needed; their type will depend on the construction material of your craft. In all cases of permanent repairs, you should follow the recommendations of the manufacturer.

CARE OF EQUIPMENT

A great deal of wear of, and general damage to, equipment is caused by improper storage, as well as outright abuse. Canoes should be evenly supported while stored, bottom up, on racks or slings, to avoid warping. Wood or plastic boats should also be sheltered from the elements. Plastics, especially, are subject to deterioration from sunlight and should be stored accordingly. You should always be careful to avoid dragging or dropping boats when you are carrying them.

All equipment (boats, paddles, ropes, life jackets, kneepads, and so on) will benefit from periodic washing and drying, especially if they are used in salt water. Life jackets especially should be thoroughly dried before they are stored. Paddles should be stored upright or hung, to prevent warping. Wooden equipment, to maintain its usefulness, requires greater care in use and storage than do other materials. Although modern plastic or metal equipment can withstand some neglect and abuse better than traditional wood can, it should obviously not be subjected to such treatment.

Paddles frequently meet with abuse when the paddler pushes off the bottom or off docks, as well as when they wear against gunwales. If you tend to drag your paddle along the gunwale in paddling, you should protect its shaft with a collar of leather or fiber glass. Exposed wood should always be touched up with varnish or boiled linseed oil to prolong its life.

Chapter 3

Fundamentals of Canoeing

This chapter is designed to present the skill and knowledge necessary for the enjoyable and safe paddling of canoes on flat water. Such water comprises lakes, bays, ponds, and other types of impoundments that do not have noticeable currents. Canals and wide, deep rivers can be used for practice, but the surface of the water must be flat. Chapters 5 and 6 cover paddling canoes on rivers with currents in excess of 1 mile per hour. Be sure that you have read Chapter 1 before you read any further.

EQUIPMENT

The Canoe

The open canoe is the craft that nearly everyone in North America associates with the name "canoe." It is a craft that when properly paddled can be used to explore remote areas of lakes and backwoods with a great deal of ease and comfort. It is ideal for flat-water paddling. (See Chapter 1, Fig. 1–3.)

The typical flat-water open canoe is pretty much a stock canoe. It can be built from aluminum, wood, or a variety of plastics. Part of the canoe's construction includes sufficient buoyancy to keep the craft afloat when it is swamped. This characteristic is an important safety feature. The amount of flotation built into a stock canoe is quite adequate for flat-water paddling.

A full-length keel is generally desirable for a flat-water canoe. Be sure yours has one. Most ABS —and some other plastic—boats have no keel, but they may have other design features that have the same function. Without a keel, most canoes will slide sideways quite readily—an undesirable feature for flat-water paddling.

Seats

Many standard canoes are equipped with seats. For lake paddling, these seats can be a blessing when long distances are involved. In the learning stages, however, kneeling is preferred for greater stability; and since solo paddling is included at this level of training, you will not always be paddling from seats in any case. *Caution:* Be aware that some manufacturers install seats quite low in some canoes. Be sure that your canoe permits your feet to be comfortably slid beneath the seat when you are kneeling and check for potentially dangerous sharp edges under the seats to avoid the possibility that your leg will be injured or your foot will be trapped. Some seats are installed quite high, which raises your center of gravity beyond a safe limit.

Kneepads

Since you will be kneeling in the canoe—for reasons of stability and leverage—you should have knee protection. Kneepads—either the wearable type or the kind that is permanently installed in the canoe—are a must. You should not paddle without them. Some experimentation with paddling positions for proper trim will be necessary before you permanently install kneepads in your canoe (Fig. 3–1).

End Lines

End lines are essential. They aid in the tying of the craft to an auto or a trailer while it is being

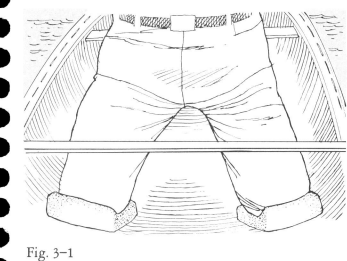

Fig. 3–1
Kneepads are essential for comfort and protection. Those shown above are glued into the canoe.

transported and in the tying off of the craft when it is in the water. They are also useful when the craft is being towed. The end lines should be at least ¼ inch in diameter, about 15 feet long, and made of good quality material, such as nylon or polypropylene. When attached to the canoe, the

end lines should be stowed, ready for use, in a place that will avoid the possibility of your becoming entangled (Fig. 3–2).

Fig. 3–2
End lines should be on both ends of all canoes and should be properly secured, ready for use.

Bailers

A bailer or a sponge should be brought along on all trips. Bailers are very useful for removing large quantities of water from the canoe. A bailer can be made from any 1-gallon plastic jug if you cut off the bottom. (Make sure you keep the cap on.) A sponge is quite useful for removing small quantities of water, especially from hard-to-reach areas.

A waterproof first aid kit should be included as well. Other equipment will depend upon the nature of the trip, and may well include waterproof containers, spare clothes, food, or other gear unrelated to paddling (Fig. 3–3).

The Paddle

For the beginning paddler, just about any paddle will do, as long as it is neither too short nor too long (Fig. 3–4). Generally, a paddle when set upright before you, should reach between your chin and your eyes. Weight, balance, integrity of construction, blade shape and size, and grip design all play an important role, although normally not

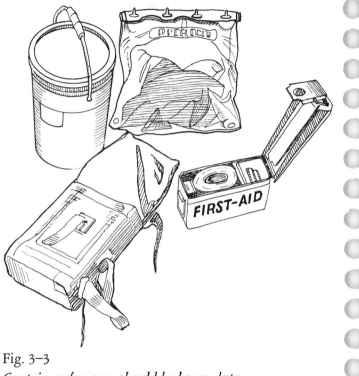

Fig. 3–3
Containers for gear should be heavy duty and waterproof.

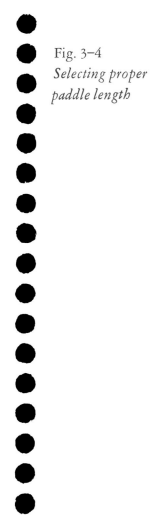

Fig. 3–4
*Selecting proper
paddle length*

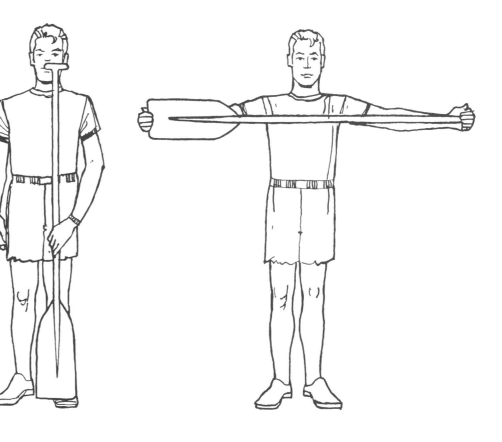

for the beginner. As you become more adept at paddling, your preferences in paddles will change; experience will dictate which paddle is best for you. Your boat should have a spare paddle aboard on any trip. Some common types of paddles are illustrated in Figure 3–5.

Paddle blades are usually 6 to 8 inches wide. If when you are paddling with the blade fully in the water the paddle seems too hard to pull or push, try a smaller blade. If the paddle moves effortlessly through the water but the canoe hardly moves, you need a wider blade. As you become more accustomed to paddling you may prefer slightly larger blades.

CLOTHING

Clothing is a very personal matter (Fig. 3–6). When selecting clothing for flat-water paddling, however, please keep in mind its insulating properties (dry and wet) and the degree to which it restricts movement (particularly at the knees and shoulders). Your comfort is the key to your ability

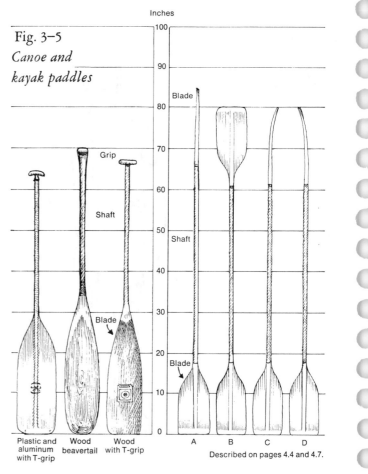

Fig. 3–5
Canoe and kayak paddles

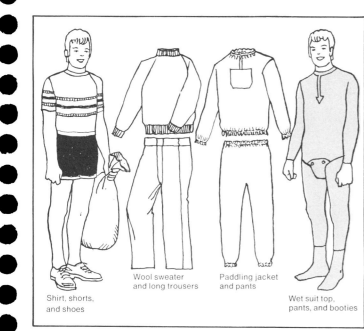

Fig. 3–6
Layers of clothing

Shirt, shorts,
and shoes

Wool sweater
and long trousers

Paddling jacket
and pants

Wet suit top,
pants, and booties

to learn and paddle effectively. As mentioned in Chapter 1, your equipment list must include a life jacket and appropriate footwear.

Footwear

Footwear is important. Without it, you subject your feet to unusual punishment. Think ahead to the time when you might have to walk or portage, then select shoes that are not only water tolerant but comfortable (wet or dry). Many consider low-top tennis shoes to be the best all-round choice.

LAUNCHING AND BOARDING

Launching and boarding your canoe have already been covered in Chapter 1, but remember these points:

- Get help and offer help to others.
- Handle your canoe by proper lifting, not by dragging.
- Have a firm grip on the canoe. You and your partner work together in lifting, carrying, and launching, and so should communicate with each other for the best teamwork.
- When there are two of you, only one person boards at a time while the other steadies the craft.

- Kneel with knees spread far apart for greater stability.
- The craft should be trimmed with the bow slightly higher than the stern.

See Figure 3–7 for boarding a canoe from a beach.

Trim and Balance

Since the canoe is supposed to remain flat while in a resting state, your position(s), whether solo or tandem, should be such that you most closely achieve this state. This goes for end-to-end trim as well as side-to-side balance. Don't be shy— move around—experiment. You will find the optimum paddling position for your circumstances —solo, tandem, or with duffel. The seats do not necessarily dictate your paddle position. Since you will be kneeling, you should lean or rest against the thwarts or seats. Also, since the canoe is double ended, either end may serve as the bow.

Fig. 3–7
Boarding a canoe from a beach

Stability

To help you develop a feel for the boat and its stability, your instructor should have you try this little drill. While in the canoe and in shallow water near shore, stow your paddle and rock the canoe from side to side, using your hips. Do not use your hands. You should be in a kneeling position with knees spread far apart and arms crossed in front of your chest or held over your head. You should be able to maintain your balance and rock the canoe enough to ship a little water over the gunwale without risking capsizing. Canoes can be very stable.

Changing Positions

Many canoe capsizings are caused when paddlers try to move about within the canoe, either when one paddler seeks to change position, or when the two paddlers try to exchange positions. Rather than the paddlers trying to exchange positions while afloat, they should paddle to shore, exit from the canoe, and then re-enter the canoe in the desired positions. Only with exceptional agility and balance can most people safely exchange positions while afloat in a canoe.

If it is necessary to move within the canoe to reach some of your stored duffel or equipment, certain procedures should be followed. First, notify your paddling partner. Stow your paddle so that both hands are free to help maintain your stability. Keep your weight low and centered over the canoe. Move slowly and deliberately.

EFFECTIVE PADDLING

The simplicity of the strokes you need to know will become apparent to you as you experiment with them. It will be more difficult, however, to achieve the finesse needed to perform these strokes efficiently. You will learn faster and with fewer frustrations under the guidance of a qualified instructor. Your instructor will probably have you perform the mechanics of the various strokes in a strictly controlled setting, using static drills. These static drills, which can take place on shore, from a dock, or with you standing in shallow water, are designed to help you "groove" the necessary movements for properly executing strokes *before* you get into the canoe. In this way, your instructor will be able to give you immediate feedback on your performance. Once you are on the water, other drills will be used to help perfect these strokes and maneuvers. Some of these drills are detailed at the end of this section (see page 3.43).

Proper hand position on the paddle is a matter of preference to experienced paddlers, but the consensus is that you should grasp the grip and shaft firmly as shown in Figure 3–8. Note that the hand on the shaft of the paddle is about 6 inches above the throat. When the paddle is held above the head, one hand on the grip, the other on the shaft, and the paddle resting on top of the head, the arms should form right angles at the elbows. This is a good rule of thumb for proper hand position on the paddle.

Another method, as shown in Figure 3-8 (b and c) is to place your hand on the shaft at the right position. In both methods, if the hand is either on the throat (the area where the paddle shaft meets the paddle blade) at the blade or more than six to eight inches up from the throat and the paddle is held as illustrated, the paddle is not the right size for you.

There are several points to be made about effective paddling. To begin with, ideally it is the canoe, not the paddle, that is moved through the water. For instance, in the forward stroke, once the paddle is inserted into the water at the begin-ning of the stroke, you and the canoe are moved to the paddle, not vice versa.

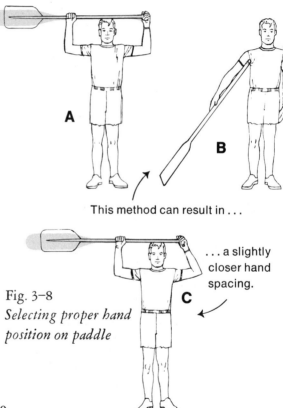

This method can result in . . .

Fig. 3–8
Selecting proper hand position on paddle

. . . a slightly closer hand spacing.

3.10

Virtually every stroke requires some body and shoulder rotation. This rotation is to your advantage because you then utilize body strength in performing the strokes, not just the arm muscles. You will find that using the recommended shoulder rotation will be less tiring than if you maintain an erect, square-shoulder posture.

Once the canoe is moving, it is relatively easy to keep it going. After starting a canoe from a standstill, try to keep the canoe moving with occasional strokes. You will find it much easier to keep the canoe moving than to wait for the canoe to glide to a stop and then get it moving again.

All strokes fall into one of two categories, those in which you "pull" on the water and those in which you "push" on the water. The face of the blade that pulls on the water is called the power face. The face of the blade that pushes on the water is called the back face. The forward stroke, the draw, and the forward sweep are examples of strokes that pull on the water using the power face. Examples of strokes that push on the water using

the back face are the back stroke, the pry, and the reverse sweep. It is important that you remember these two terms, as they will be used in descriptions of the strokes.

When paddling you should maintain a firm grasp on the shaft and grip of the paddle. This position will offer the best control of the paddle. The hand and arm holding the shaft are often referred to as the lower hand or the lower arm. The "top arm" and "grip hand" are those on the grip of the paddle. Again, these terms are often used in descriptions of the various paddling strokes.

The recovery of the paddle, whether through the air or through the water after completion of a stroke, must be done in such a way as to minimize resistance against the paddle. This maneuver is called feathering. It means, simply, to rotate the paddle, back face toward the water (Fig. 3–9), during the recovery of the paddle from the end of one stroke to the beginning of another. On some occasions you will find it advantageous to recover

Fig. 3–9
Feathering the blade during recovery

underwater by rotating the paddle and slicing the blade through the water directly to the beginning of another stroke. Relaxation during the recovery is most important in reducing fatigue. Each recovery should be done in a very relaxed manner, as this is the only opportunity for rest during paddling. If your muscles are always tense during the recovery, you will become fatigued unnecessarily.

It should be made clear that in actual practice, strokes are modified or combined to produce a desired movement or reaction of the canoe, rather than always used in a pure form, as presented here. However, you must be able to get as much as possible out of each stroke in its pure form before you can effectively modify or combine strokes. After the strokes are presented and developed in their pure form, you will begin to try some simple maneuvers that require the modifying and combining of these strokes.

The Strokes

The most important strokes in paddling are described below. Certain combinations of these strokes will not be detailed here, but some of these combinations—and their components—are listed in the next section.

When you are first introduced to these strokes, solo paddling will be stressed, because by this means you will more readily learn how the canoe responds to each stroke. After you become familiar with the strokes and the response of the canoe, you will be better prepared to develop the teamwork needed to effectively paddle in tandem.

STROKES

The Forward Stroke

Purpose. To move the canoe forward.

Description. The paddle enters the water comfortably ahead of the paddler's position. The body —especially the shoulders—is rotated, with the lower arm extended and its shoulder leading. The top arm is cocked and near the head.

With the blade perpendicular to the keel line and the paddle vertical (grip over the water), pull straight along the side of the canoe parallel to the keel line. Power is applied with the top arm punching forward and down, over the blade, as the lower arm pulls. The body follows through by rotating to let the top arm and its shoulder lead. Body and shoulder rotation provides much of the power.

The stroke ends as the top arm is fully extended with the lower hand near the hip. Recovery begins when the blade is just behind the hip, with the paddler slicing the blade out of the water in an arc toward the bow. The paddler then feathers the blade to the start of a new stroke.

Synopsis. The tendency of the bow will be to turn away from the paddling side, especially if the paddle is not vertical or close to the side of the canoe during the stroke. Repeated strokes will result in increased speed (to a point) and increased turning. A large circle should result (Fig. 3–10).

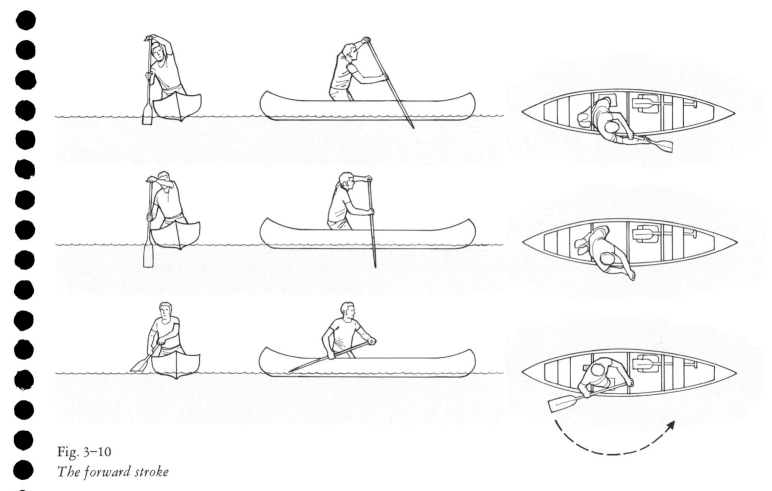

Fig. 3–10
The forward stroke

The Backstroke

Purpose. To stop the forward motion of the canoe or to move it backward.

Description. The blade enters the water just behind the paddler and is flat to the surface. The paddler's body is rotated toward the paddling side, with the grip hand out over the water, arm extended. The bottom hand is next to the hip.

The paddle moves forward along the side of the canoe, parallel to the keel line, and power is applied to the stroke. The lower arm pushes down and forward as the top arm and its shoulder pull up and back, keeping the grip over the water. Shoulder rotation is most useful at the beginning of the stroke, and the arms follow through toward the end.

The stroke ends comfortably in front of the paddler, with the lower arm extended forward and the top arm bent, with the grip near the head. The paddler slices the blade out of the water and feathers to the beginning of a new stroke.

Synopsis. The canoe will move backward, with the bow tending to turn toward the paddle side, especially if the grip is not kept out over the water during the stroke. Repeated strokes will result in more speed (to a point) and more turning. A large circle should result (Fig. 3–11).

Fig. 3–11

The backstroke

The Drawstroke

Purpose. To move the canoe sideways toward the paddle.

Description. The paddle enters the water directly to the side of the paddler, blade parallel to the keel line. The paddler's body is rotated toward the paddle side, with the lower arm nearly extended and the top arm cocked over the head.

The paddle pulls with the power face toward the canoe, perpendicular to the keel line, with the blade kept parallel to the keel line as power is applied. The top arm punches out over the water as the lower arm pulls toward the canoe. The shoulders rotate until parallel with the keel line. The paddle should remain nearly vertical throughout the stroke.

Recovery begins when the paddle is about 6 inches from the side of the canoe as the top arm is extended out over the water and the bent lower arm is near the side. The paddler may either slice the blade out of the water toward the stern by lowering the grip hand, or may slice the blade through the water directly to the start of a new draw by rotating the paddle 90 degrees (power face aft—near or toward the stern) and feathering through the water. The paddler should not let the paddle hit the side of the canoe before recovery begins.

Synopsis. The canoe should move directly sideways toward the paddling side, with no turning. During the stroke the boat may have a tendency to lean away from the paddling side (Fig. 3–12).

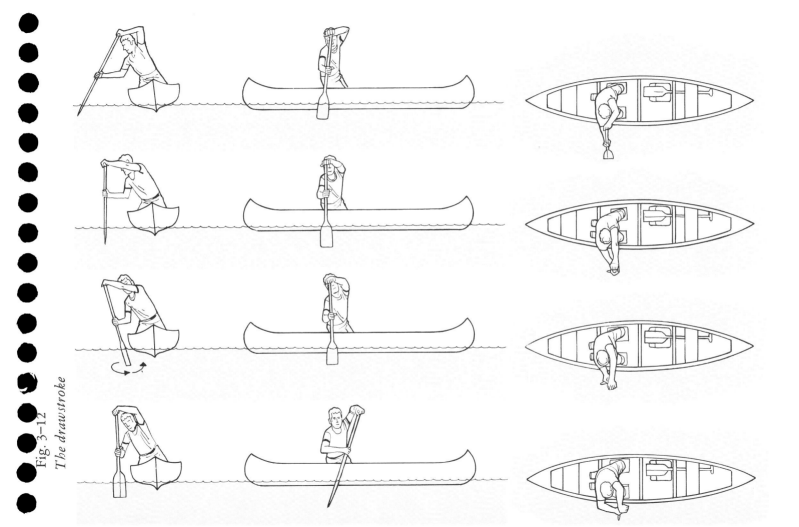

Fig. 3-12 *The drawstroke*

The Pushaway Stroke

Purpose. To move the canoe sideways away from the paddle.

Description. The paddle enters the water directly alongside the paddler, with the blade just under the bilge (the area where the bottom of the boat meets the side of the boat) and parallel to the keel line. The shoulders are rotated toward the paddle side, with the top arm extended out over the water and the lower arm bent and braced against the paddler's side.

The paddle pushes with the back face away from the canoe perpendicular to the keel line, with the blade parallel to it as power is applied. The top arm and shoulder pull in toward the center of the canoe while the lower arm acts as a fulcrum initially and pushes out over the water near the end of the stroke. The paddle should be nearly vertical throughout the stroke.

Recovery begins as the lower arm is extended out over the water a comfortable distance from the side of the canoe. The paddler can make the recovery either by lifting the blade from the water and swinging it toward the stern to begin another pushaway or by rotating the paddle 90 degrees (power face aft) and slicing it directly to the beginning of a new pushaway through the water.

Synopsis. The canoe should move directly sideways away from the paddling side with no turning. The canoe may tend to tilt or lean toward the paddling side during this stroke (Fig. 3–13).

Fig. 3–13
The pushaway stroke

The Pry Stroke

Purpose. To forcefully move the canoe sideways away from the paddling side.

Description. The paddle enters the water directly alongside the paddler, with the blade extended under the bilge, the shaft against the side of the canoe. The body is rotated toward the paddle side as the lower arm keeps the shaft in contact with the canoe. The top arm is extended well out over the water.

The blade, while kept parallel to the keel line, pushes with the back face away from the canoe, perpendicular to the keel line. The top arm and shoulder pull in toward the center of the canoe in a prying action, with the side of the canoe acting as the fulcrum. The paddle should be nearly vertical throughout.

Recovery begins with the shaft still in contact with the side of the canoe as the grip comes in front of the paddler's chest. The blade should be only a short distance from the side of the canoe. The blade may be rotated or it may be sliced out of the water and swung in an arc toward the stern to begin another pry.

Synopsis. The canoe should move directly sideways away from the paddling side with no turning. This stroke has a tendency to tip the canoe toward the paddle side, especially if the pry is carried too far from the side of the canoe (Fig. 3–14).

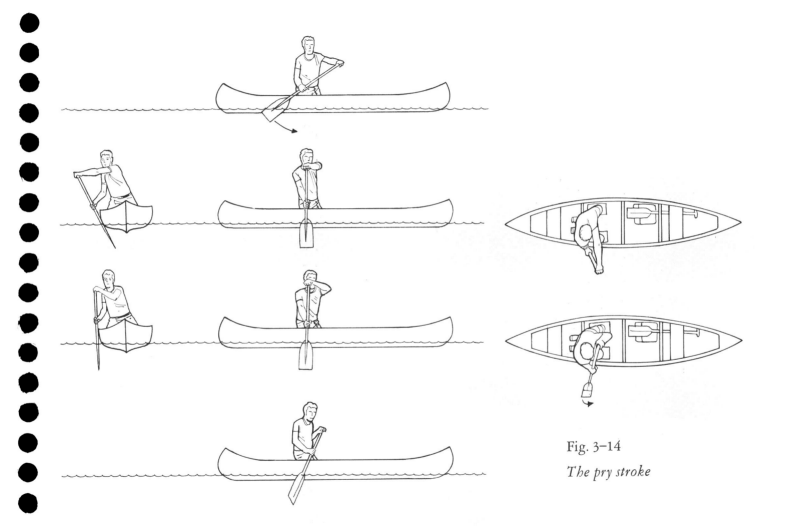

Fig. 3–14

The pry stroke

The Forward Sweep

Purpose. To move the canoe forward and turn the bow away from the paddling side.

Description. The blade enters the water well forward of the paddler, alongside the canoe, with the blade vertical and the paddle nearly horizontal. The paddler leans forward, the lower arm extended and its shoulder rotated forward. The grip hand is low and in front of the body.

With the power face, the blade is pulled out from the bow and around toward the stern in a large arc of nearly 180 degrees. Power is applied by the lower arm and its shoulder pulling the paddle through its arc as the grip arm pushes forward and out over the water from in front of the body. The shoulders should rotate at least 90 degrees during this stroke.

The stroke ends nearly under the stern of the canoe, with the grip hand extended out over the water and the paddler's upper torso facing the paddling side. The lower arm is extended toward the stern, well behind the paddler. The paddler makes the recovery by lifting the blade out of the water and swinging it feathered in an arc to the start of another stroke.

Synopsis. The canoe should turn sharply, bow away from the paddling side, with very little headway (forward movement). Repeated strokes will result in a very tight circle, with the canoe moving forward and the bow turning away from the paddling side (Fig. 3-15).

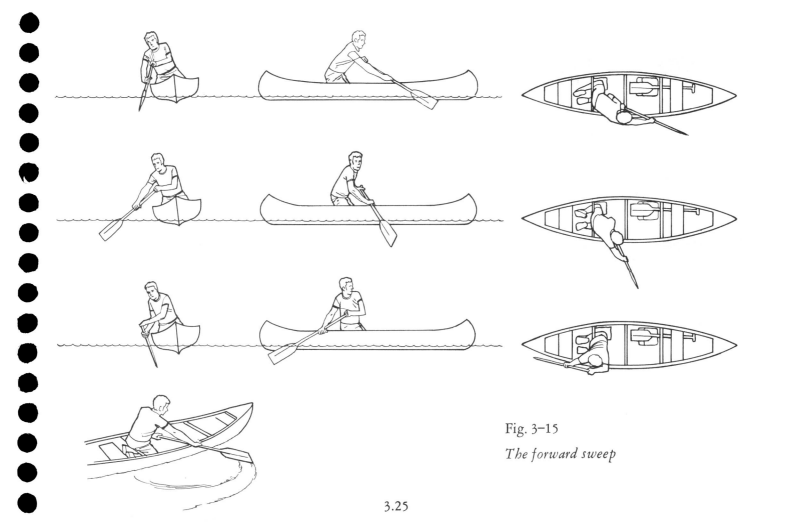

Fig. 3–15

The forward sweep

3.25

The Reverse Sweep

Purpose. To turn the bow sharply toward the paddling side and reduce headway or move backward.

Description. The blade enters the water well behind the paddler, with the blade vertical, paddle nearly horizontal and extended well astern. The paddler's body is rotated toward the paddling side, leaning aft, with the lower arm nearly extended toward the stern and the grip hand alongside the hips and out over the water.

The back face pushes against the water as the paddle is moved through a broad arc of nearly 180 degrees toward the bow. Power is applied with the lower arm pushing the blade, first out and then toward the bow as the shoulders rotate at 90 degrees. The grip hand pulls in toward the abdomen and stays just above gunwale level throughout.

Recovery begins with the paddle near the bow as the body is leaning slightly forward, with the lower arm extended and its shoulder leading toward the bow. The paddler completes the recovery by lifting the blade out of the water and swinging it in an arc to the beginning of another stroke, with the blade feathered.

Synopsis. The canoe should turn sharply, bow toward the paddling side, with a slight amount of sternway (backward movement). Repeated strokes will result in a very tight circle, bow toward the paddle, with slight sternway (Fig. 3-16).

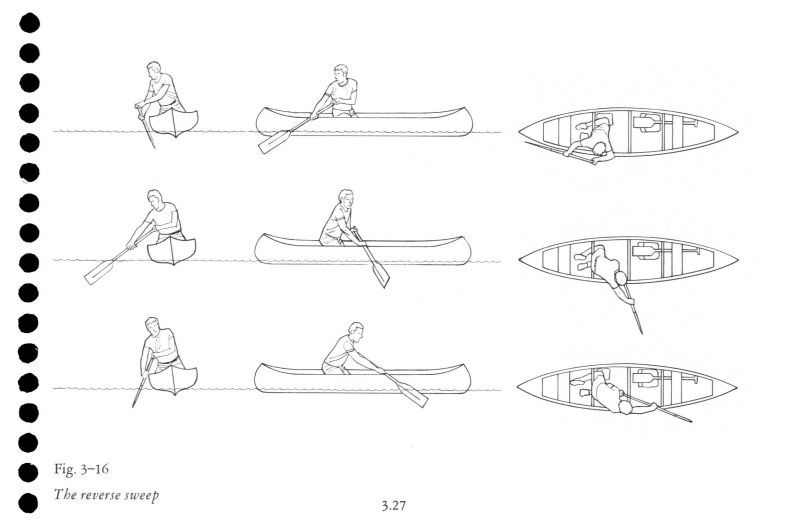

Fig. 3–16

The reverse sweep

3.27

The Cross Draw

Purpose. To turn the bow away from the paddling side and reduce headway.

Description. The stroke begins at the side of the bow opposite the normal paddling side *without the paddler's changing the grasp of the paddle* (Fig. 3–17A). The body is rotated sharply away from the paddle side, with the lower arm extended forward and out over the water. The grip hand is cocked and near the paddler's side as the vertical blade enters the water about 2 feet from the bow and well forward of the paddler's position.

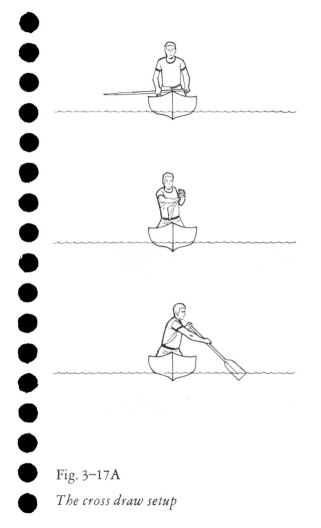

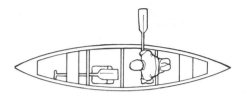

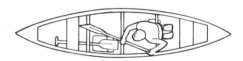

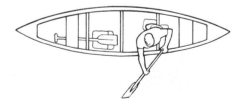

Fig. 3–17A

The cross draw setup

3.29

With the power face, the blade moves in a short arc directly toward the side of the canoe forward of the paddler. Power is applied by the grip hand, which punches out over the water as the lower arm pulls in toward the canoe. Shoulder rotation provides additional power as the bottom arm remains extended.

Recovery begins as the paddle reaches the side of the canoe and the grip hand is out over the water. The blade is lifted up out of the water and swung, feathered, in an arc to the start of another stroke.

Synopsis. The bow will swing abruptly away from the normal paddling side as headway is reduced. Repeated strokes will continue to turn the bow and add slight sternway (Fig. 3–17B).

The description of the basic strokes in their pure form is now complete. The purpose of the presentation is to facilitate your understanding of the principles involved, so that you will be better able to modify and combine these strokes to meet your specific needs.

In the next section some specific maneuvers are presented that will require the modification or combination of strokes already described. A few additional strokes will also be presented: stationary strokes and the stern rudder. Some other strokes—namely, the compound backstroke, low brace, and high brace—are described in Chapter 5, "Basic River Canoeing."

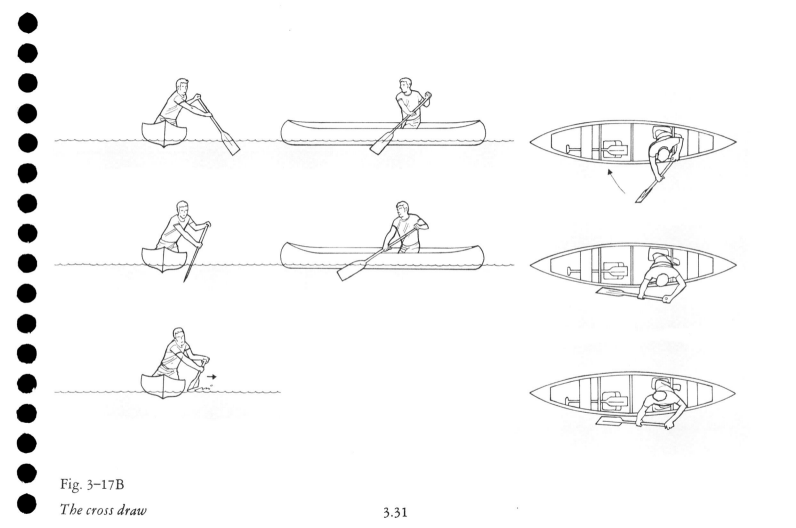

Fig. 3–17B

The cross draw

3.31

Maneuvers

The last section dealt with pure strokes. This section deals with combinations of strokes that are used for canoe control and specific maneuvers: pivot turns, sideslipping, and paddling a straight line.

Maneuvering a canoe takes practice and an understanding of all the strokes described in the previous section. When these strokes are combined in various ways, you can make the canoe do just about any maneuver you can think of. To become a proficient paddler you must learn to combine strokes and apply them in new ways to make the canoe perform in the desired manner.

To improve your understanding of how to control the canoe, you might find the concept of the "turning circle" helpful. Keep in mind that a canoe does not steer like a car, it turns around a pivot point near the center of the canoe. Therefore, as one end of the canoe turns in one direction, the other end will go in the opposite direction. Imagine yourself alone in your canoe doing a for-

ward sweep. You are the pivot point, and the blade of the paddle goes in a circular path from the bow to the stern. The bow turns away from the paddle as the stern turns toward it (Fig. 3–18).

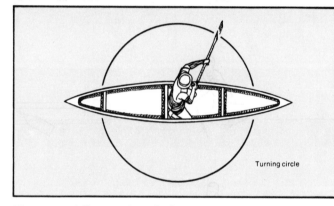

Fig. 3–18 *The turning circle*

Your paddle has moved along the turning circle. Using strokes along the turning circle is, generally, the most efficient way to turn the canoe. Virtually every possible maneuver requires turning the canoe. Even going straight requires turning. An extreme case of turning is a pivot turn.

Each of the following maneuvers is described for both solo and tandem paddling. The advantage of solo paddling is that you can do it when there is no one else available to paddle with you. In a learning situation the advantage of solo paddling is that you know that whatever happens to the canoe is the result of your action or inaction and no one else's.

Tandem paddling, however, has the advantage that there is someone to help with the physical task of controlling the canoe, as well as someone to help think of solutions to problems that may develop. To effectively paddle in tandem, it is important that you effectively communicate your intentions to each other. To simplify things, it is best to arbitrarily designate one person as being in command. Remember that each of you shares responsibility for what happens in the canoe, and each is responsible for controlling his end of the canoe for each maneuver.

Pivot Turns

The purpose of a pivot turn is to make a canoe turn around with no headway or sternway. The canoe should remain in place and rotate bow for stern. When you practiced forward and reverse sweeps, alone in your canoe, you made tight turns, but they were not quite pivot turns because you had a little headway or sternway. There are two commonly used techniques for solo pivot turns: the outside pivot and the inside pivot.

The outside pivot turn is the easier of the two turns, since it combines two basic strokes, the cross draw and the forward sweep. Start with a cross draw and follow immediately with a forward sweep (Fig. 3–19).

The paddle recovery is the same as that for a full sweep except that you would recover to a new cross-draw entry. Three or four good strokes should pivot your canoe 360 degrees.

The inside pivot turn is a little more complicated. The stroke begins as a reverse sweep, with the back face of the blade. Halfway through the stroke the blade is turned so that the power face of the blade is used to finish the stroke in a drawing action,

3.33

Fig. 3–19
The outside pivot turn combines the cross draw and the forward sweep.

reverse sweep; (2) rotate the blade; (3) do a bow draw; (4) do a diagonal drawstroke at the beginning of the recovery; and (5) recover through the water to the beginning position. The position of your hands does not change. A firm grasp on the paddle throughout the stroke is essential. Also, you will notice that the recovery is short and through the water after the drawstroke. All actions are designed to pivot the canoe with little or no fore or aft movement (Fig. 3–20).

Pivot turns in tandem can be performed in a variety of ways—and with greater ease than solo turns, as each paddler is responsible for moving only his end of the canoe, not the whole canoe. A very common and effective combination is for you and your partner to use drawstrokes (Fig. 3–21). In this case your drawstrokes should be along the turning circle. Pry strokes or pushaways can be used to pivot in the other direction.

As part of a tandem crew you can also combine forward and reverse sweeps to pivot the canoe (Fig. 3–22). As an example, you do the forward

which continues in an arc toward the bow. Since a reverse sweep provides some sternway, modified draws are used to continue the turn and to counter the slight sternway. The sequence is (1) do a

Fig. 3–20
The inside pivot turn combines the reverse sweep and the drawstroke.

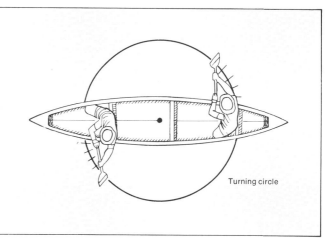

Fig. 3–21
Drawstrokes in tandem, to pivot the canoe

sweep and your partner does a reverse sweep, or vice versa. In tandem paddling, your sweep strokes are shortened (to an arc of about 90 degrees, not 180 degrees), since each of you is responsible for turning only your end of the canoe. You use the end of the stroke along the turning circle at your end of the canoe. If you carry your strokes toward the center of the canoe you will leave the turning circle and will not turn the canoe. With a little experimentation, you and your partner may discover many combinations of strokes that can pivot your canoe effectively.

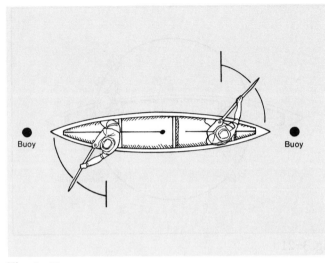

Fig. 3–22
Sweeps (forward and reverse) in tandem, to pivot the canoe. Note that the strokes go through only a 90-degree arc.

Drills. To help you develop greater proficiency in these maneuvers, your instructor may provide some drills that use aids such as buoys. You can also set up your own aids to practice with on your own. For your pivot turns, a buoy that is station-ary on the water is needed. With this aid you will be able to observe foreward or backward move-ment of the canoe. Highly proficient paddlers are able to pivot their canoe within a circle only slightly larger than the length of the canoe. As an example, set out two buoys on the water so that the distance between them is slightly greater than the length of the canoe. Do your pivot turn between the buoys without touching them and staying directly between them. Four buoys could also be used.

Sideslipping

Sideslipping is a maneuver that moves the canoe sideways. A canoe at rest on the water is easily moved sideways by drawstrokes, pry strokes, or pushaways. Sideslipping can also be done as the canoe moves forward. However, you will find it more efficient to take advantage of the canoe's headway by using stationary strokes rather than drawstrokes, pry strokes, or pushaways.

Stationary strokes rely upon the canoe's moving through the water as the blade is held in a fixed position relative to the boat and paddler. As the boat slows down, the strokes lose power. Once headway is lost, power strokes such as draws and pry strokes must be used for additional sideways movement.

Stationary draw. This maneuver starts the same as a drawstroke except that—

1. The forward, or leading, edge of the blade is angled away from the keel line at 30 to 45 degrees.

2. The paddle is held in place with the blade fully immersed in the water (Fig. 3–23).

Stationary pry. This stroke starts the same as a pry stroke except that—

1. The forward, or leading, edge of the blade is angled toward the keel line at 30 to 45 degrees.

2. The paddle is held in place with the blade fully immersed in the water (see Fig. 3–23).

Stern rudder. This stroke is used by the stern paddler in a tandem crew. The paddle is held in place as if slightly into a reverse sweep, with the paddle nearly horizontal and at about a 30-degree angle to the keel line. With the bow paddler doing

Fig. 3–23 *Sideslipping a moving canoe with the stationary draw (stern) and stationary pry (bow) strokes*

3.37

a stationary draw at the same time, the canoe can be made to move sideways without turning (Fig. 3–24). As you and your partner practice, the stern paddler can sight along the canoe and vary the angle of his paddle to keep the canoe on line. It is useful to set out a buoy and sideslip around it to practice this maneuver.

The Duffek (du' fek)

The Duffek is an efficient combination of strokes that is used to sharply turn the moving canoe 90 degrees or more and maintain headway. It combines a stationary draw, a high brace, a draw toward the bow, and a forward stroke (Fig. 3–25).

Paddling a Straight Line—Forward

As you noticed with the forward stroke, in paddling solo or in tandem, the canoe does not go straight, it always tends to turn away from the stern paddler's side. Most novices will correct by changing paddling sides every few strokes. This is a popular technique among some racers and can be quite efficient because it utilizes only pure for-

Fig. 3–24

A stern rudder and a stationary draw, to sideslip the canoe

3.38

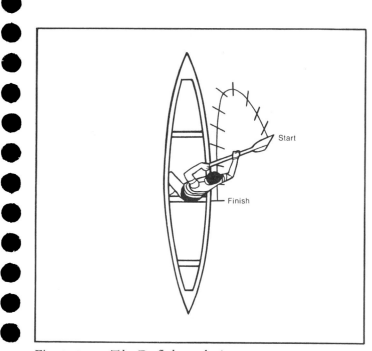

Fig. 3–25   *The Duffek stroke in a canoe*

ward strokes. However, you should be able to control your canoe by utilizing some compound strokes, such as those described below.

Rudder. One method is to drag the blade through the water as a rudder. This technique is very inefficient, since dragging the blade acts as a brake.

The pry. A more efficient technique is to do a crisp, short pry at the end of the forward stroke, as needed, to correct for the tendency of the boat to turn. The pry should be short, quick, with the back face, and right under the side of the canoe aft of the paddler, for best effect. The thumb of the grip hand is turned up. This technique is popular in whitewater, where powerful course corrections are often required (Fig. 3–26).

The hook-J. Even more efficient is the hook-J, in which the power face is used throughout the stroke. The "hook" action is at the end and pushes out and away from the stern to steer the canoe. The thumb on the grip is turned down (Fig. 3–27).

The pitch-J. Another technique is the pitch-J. In this stroke, as the paddle moves aft, the blade is "pitched," or turned, at an angle to the keel line (the inside edge leading to the stern), with the power face being used throughout. The path of

Fig. 3–26
*The pry at the end of a forward stroke, to
maintain a straight course*

Fig. 3–27
The hook-J stroke

the paddle can actually be straight, with no hook
or J. This stroke provides constant headway, as it
corrects the course and can be done in cadence
with your bow partner. Again, the thumb of the
grip hand is turned down (Fig. 3–28).

In solo paddling. All these techniques for
straight-line paddling can be improved by the
paddler's using a slight draw at the catch of the
stroke. In solo paddling, the steering portion of
the stroke must occur aft of the paddler, otherwise

Fig. 3–28
The pitch-J stroke

the canoe may move sideways instead of turning back onto course.

For tandem use. The strokes remain essentially the same. Note that these strokes would be used only by the stern paddler. One exception is that no draw should be done at the beginning of the stroke. Another is that the steering part of the stroke (pry, hook, or pitch) can occur earlier during the stroke with no adverse effects.

Practice. Once you have developed some ability to keep the canoe on a straight course, you should refine this skill by practicing along a stationary reference, such as the edge of a dock, shore line, or buoyed rope. Highly proficient paddlers can paddle a straight line even through a narrow channel only slightly wider than the canoe (Fig. 3–29).

Dock or buoyed line

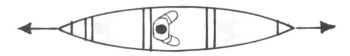

Fig. 3–29

A practice drill for straight line paddling either solo (solid figure) or tandem (shaded figures)

Paddling a Straight Line—Backward

It is also necessary to keep your canoe on a straight course when it is moving backward. This can be accomplished by the use of a pry at the end of a backstroke. The thumb on the grip hand should turn down to put the back face into position for the pry. It should be noted that with the canoe moving backward, and the stern trimmed lower in the water than the bow, the canoe will tend to turn, in any direction. Thus, as you paddle backward, it will sometimes be necessary to use a pry to turn the canoe back onto course, and at other times it will be necessary to use a reverse sweep or a draw (Fig. 3–30).

When paddling in tandem, the bow paddler is responsible for keeping the canoe on course. For more drastic course changes or corrections the stern paddler should assist.

SKILLS PRACTICE

Included in this section are many drills that will enable you to refine the strokes and maneuvers you

Fig. 3–30
A pry used to steer a straight course backward

have learned in this chapter. However, to do so without the able assistance of a qualified instructor could prove difficult. Even though the descriptions and the illustrations are accurate, you may begin to develop bad habits that could be hard to correct at a later date. Try to develop proficiency in all strokes on each side of a canoe. In the beginning stages, practice out of the wind in a sheltered area.

Drills

Wiggle course. Paddle through the buoys without touching them (Fig. 3–31).

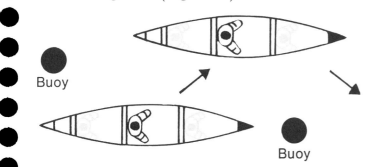

Buoy

Buoy

Fig. 3–31
A "wiggle" course for sideslipping

Dock landing. Do a last-minute 90-degree turn and stop at arm's reach. Do not touch the dock. Select a specific target for the middle thwart to stop at. Note the straight path of the middle thwart (Fig. 3–32).

Sideways. Practice lateral moves along a buoyed rope or dock by means of draws, pry strokes, or pushaways. Keep close to the rope and maintain the same angle to it, either 90 degrees or 45 degrees, without turning (Fig. 3–33).

Corner drill. Paddle around a buoy at a corner; paddle toward the buoy and do a 90-degree turn without hitting the outside of the corner or losing speed (Fig. 3–34).

Back and forth. In a corridor defined by a buoyed rope, paddle straight forward, stop, and paddle back without turning or drifting into the buoyed rope.

Series of gates. Set up gates as shown (Fig. 3–35) and paddle various courses through them. Two such courses are suggested. If you are learning to paddle with other people, try taking turns and timing how long it takes to complete a specified course. This is not only a challenge but fun and highly educational (Fig. 3–36).

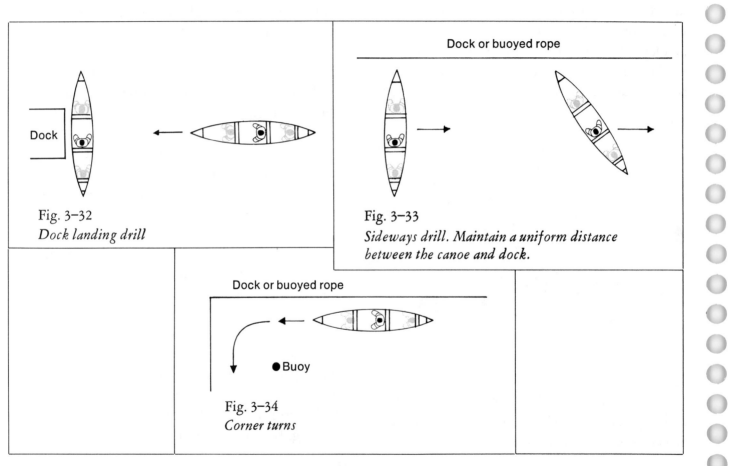

Dock

Fig. 3–32
Dock landing drill

Dock or buoyed rope

Fig. 3–33
*Sideways drill. Maintain a uniform distance
between the canoe and dock.*

Dock or buoyed rope

● Buoy

Fig. 3–34
Corner turns

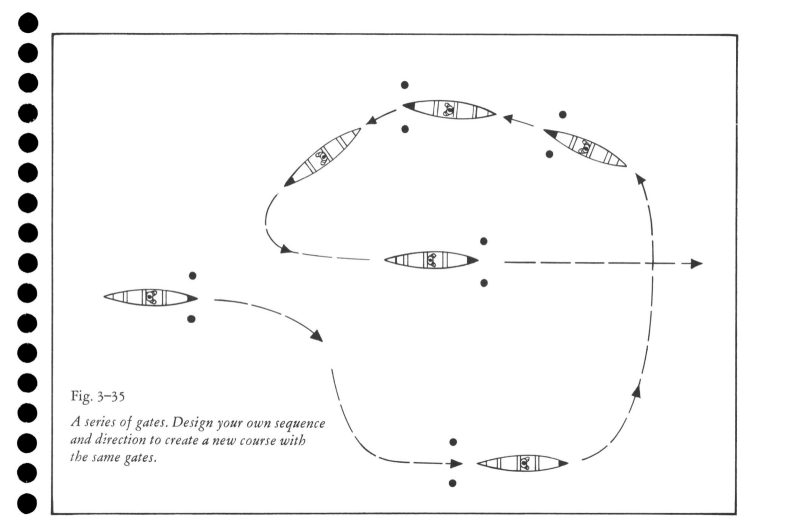

Fig. 3–35

A series of gates. Design your own sequence and direction to create a new course with the same gates.

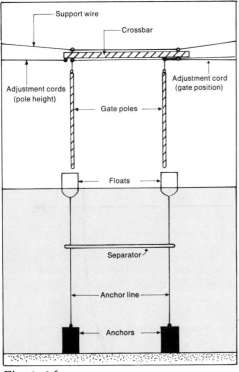

Fig. 3–36
Construction details for a hung and a floating gate. Make wide gates for beginners, narrow ones for more experienced paddlers.

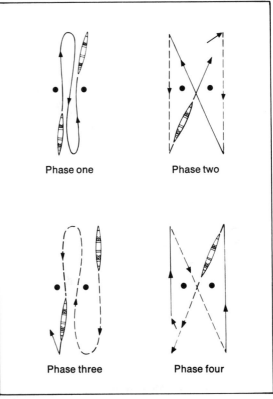

Phase one   Phase two

Phase three   Phase four

Fig. 3–37
The English gate

The English gate. The English gate is a series of passes through a gate 4 to 6 feet wide. This series of maneuvers calls upon all of the skills taught in this chapter. It is an ideal training exercise, especially when you time yourself and attempt to complete the required maneuvers in successively shorter times. The English gate is described in four phases (Fig. 3–37):

Phase 1:

Start when bow enters gate.
1. Pass through gate forward.
2. Turn around (right).
3. Pass through gate forward.
4. Turn around (left).
5. Pass through gate forward.

Phase 2:

1. Pass outside right of gate backward.
2. Pass through gate forward.
3. Pass outside left of gate backward.
4. Pass through gate forward.

Phase 3:

1. Pass outside right of gate backward.
2. Turn around left.
3. Pass through gate backward.
4. Turn around right.
5. Pass through gate backward.

Phase 4:

1. Pass outside left of gate forward.
2. Pass through gate backward.
3. Pass outside right of gate forward.
4. Pass through gate backward.

Finish when bow leaves gate.

Needless to say, you should try not to touch the buoys that make up the gate. A true test of your ability is to add 10 seconds to your elapsed time for each touch and still get through the entire exercise in under 240 seconds, or 4 minutes (elapsed time plus penalties). Experts can not only complete the exercise clean (no touches), but do it in less than 110 seconds.

In general, any of the drills used above—or drills of your own design—will help dramatically in improving your skills, either solo or tandem. As a rule, the faster the time, the better your skill. However, you cannot expect an 18-foot canoe with a deep keel to be as maneuverable a craft as a keelless 15-foot canoe.

RESCUE

Your instruction in paddling has not been completed until you are capable of handling the routine mishaps that occur as part of the sport. The most common mishap for a canoeist is to end up in the water, either by falling overboard, capsizing, or swamping. You should be able not only to handle your own craft in these cases, but to assist others in need. Being prepared by expecting any one of these events to occur is the first step in handling the mishap. *Always be prepared to swim.*

There are several things you can do to be better prepared for a mishap. These include the selection of appropriate apparel and equipment, as well as

the mastery of techniques for self-rescue and the rescue of others. Equipment and apparel have been discussed earlier, but remember:

- Clothing should be selected for its ability to keep you warm and comfortable when you are wet.
- Take warm dry clothes along in a waterproof container.
- Carry all recommended equipment, including a repair kit, a first aid kit, a throw rope, extra flotation gear, bailers, and spare paddles.

It is best to be aware of your abilities and limitations, as well as those of your craft, under a variety of conditions. Finally, you must practice all the skills described here, on a regular basis.

Self-Rescue

The simplest form of self-rescue is appropriate only when the water is relatively warm and safety is nearby. That method is for you to hang onto your craft and swim it and yourself to shore, as described in Chapter 1. Do not leave your canoe. It is easier to spot a canoe than it is to spot you alone in the water. In addition, a canoe provides valuable buoyancy.

If you have fallen out of the canoe, it is easy to re-enter the empty canoe as shown (Fig. 3–38):
- Use your hands on the bottom of the canoe.
- Push and kick until your hips are over the gunwale.
- Roll onto your back.
- Swing your legs on board last of all.

If your canoe is swamped you can hand-paddle to shore. If you are not already in the canoe, the technique you use to re-enter is similar to the one you use in re-entering your empty canoe. The key points (Fig. 3–39) are as follows:
- One person re-enters at a time.
- Do not push the gunwales far below the surface.
- Keep your weight low in the canoe.
- Go slowly, one step at a time.

Once at shore you can empty water from your swamped canoe in a variety of ways. It can be done at shore, at a dock, or in deep water. If you

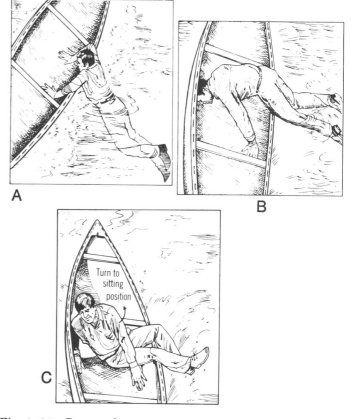

Fig. 3–38 *Re-entering an empty canoe*

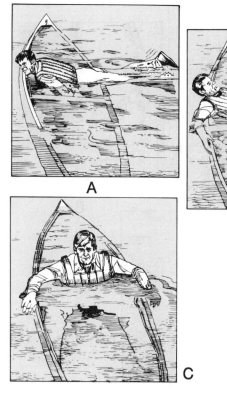

Fig. 3–39
Re-entering a swamped canoe

have a swamped canoe in shallow water, it can be emptied as shown in Chapter 1, page 1.19.

Anytime you end up in cold water some distance from shore, it is best to get back into an empty canoe before hypothermia sets in. If assistance is not available, you will need to perform the Capistrano flip.

The Capistrano Flip

The Capistrano flip is a quick self-rescue technique based on emptying water from a swamped canoe in deep water. It is best performed by two or more people wearing life jackets. After the canoe has been swamped, it is turned upside down, with a large air pocket underneath. You and your partner under the boat in unison lift one gunwale to break the suction, and *quickly* throw the canoe up and over (Fig. 3–40). Timing, strength, and coordination are vital, but even when the maneuver is poorly executed, enough water is removed to permit ready bailing. You may then re-enter the emptied canoe (see Fig. 3–38). This technique works best when the swamped canoe has good

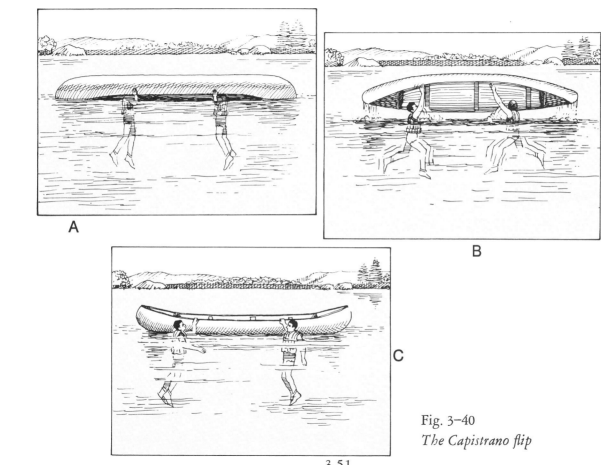

A

B

C

Fig. 3-40
The Capistrano flip

3.51

buoyancy. Large end tanks are very good for providing such buoyancy. If you cannot do a Capistrano flip with your canoe, consider adding flotation gear until you can do it.

It is always best to be self-sufficient in your participation in canoeing, rather than dependent on others for your safety and well-being. Practice these self-rescue skills until you have confidence in them.

Rescue of Others

As a member of a paddling group, you should be prepared to lend assistance to anyone else in the group. The group is strongest when all members are capable of self-rescue, but a helping hand is always welcome.

Extension Rescue

When you are assisting a person in the water, it is necessary to avoid getting into the water yourself. The best way to avoid doing so is by extending your reach from shore, for example, by using a throw rope.

The *throw rope bag* is probably the most versatile of extension aids. It enables you to extend your reach to the full length of the rope or to use any shorter length that is needed.

The bag shown (Fig. 3–41) is of particular importance. It keeps 50 to 75 feet of ⅜-inch floatable polypropylene rope tangle-free and ready to throw at all times. The simplicity of its use makes this rope ideal. Every boat should have one of these.

The diagram below shows the construction of the bag. The resilient foam disk gives the bag its shape and provides enough flotation to prevent the bag from sinking and becoming caught on some obstruction.

The victim's end of the rope is secured to the bag through the disk. During loading of the bag, the rope is fed into the bag and allowed to collect naturally—*do not coil the rope in the bag*. The loop on the rescuer's end of the rope is kept outside the bag, and the mouth of the bag is pulled closed with a drawstring. The drawstring is then

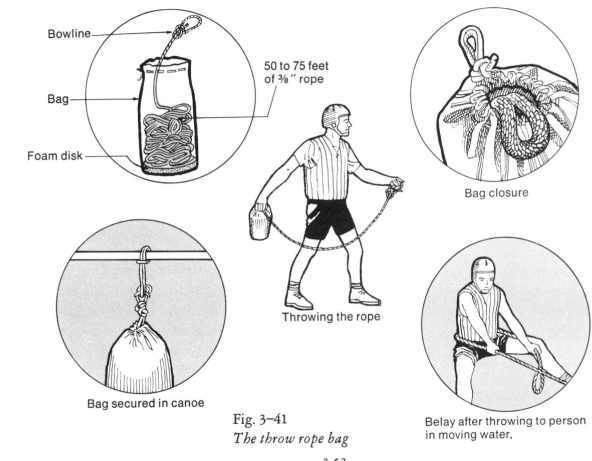

Bowline

Bag

50 to 75 feet
of ⅜″ rope

Foam disk

Bag closure

Throwing the rope

Bag secured in canoe

Belay after throwing to person
in moving water.

Fig. 3–41
The throw rope bag

3.53

loosely tied. With the mouth of the bag closed there should still be about a 1-inch opening for the rope to feed out. The rescuer's loop is a grab loop only, not a wrist loop.

To use the throw bag, simply grab the loop and bag as shown and toss the bag. The rope will feed out of the bag smoothly. Your toss can be underarm, sidearm, or overarm, depending upon obstructions and the way you prefer to throw.

If you miss, haul the bag in quickly, letting the rope collect at your feet. Take care not to step on or tangle the coils. The bag will usually pick up some water. This water adds weight, enabling you to throw the bag again without restuffing the rope into the bag. The weighted bag will pull the rope at your feet out full length once again. However, if the bag is too heavy, some water must be emptied from the bag. Experience is your best guide.

Other types of rescue ropes can be used quite successfully, but the rescuer must have greater strength and better coordination to use them.

Other forms of extensions can be branches, clothing, or paddles. These extensions can be used from a canoe, but remember that you are less stable in a canoe than on shore. In all forms of extension rescues, you need to be in a braced and stable position to avoid being pulled into trouble. Remember, the idea is to extend your reach without getting into the water and endangering yourself.

Assisting Others From Your Boat

In addition to assisting others from the shore, you can do so from your boat.

Flotation aid. If the victim is not wearing a life jacket, the first thing to do is to throw one to him or have him put on one that may be nearby. In addition, have him hang on to his capsized boat if it is nearby. Under no circumstance should a victim swim to you without some flotation device. His energy should be spent in staying afloat, and you should go to him.

Towing. Simply present the stern of your boat to the victim and tow him to shore. This maneuver does take strength and some paddling skill, and you should therefore not attempt these rescues if you cannot successfully complete them. Instead, use your throw bag from shore.

Re-entry. It may be possible for the victim to climb aboard your canoe if the water is not too rough (see page 3.49). A second boat could come alongside yours for you to brace gunwales together to provide greater stability (see canoe-over-canoe rescue, below). Should the victim have his boat in tow, you can either nudge the swamped boat with yours or struggle through by pulling the victim and his boat to shore. Remember, if the water is cold, get the victim or victims out of the water as soon as possible.

In using your canoe to assist persons in the water, you must take several precautions. First, as you approach them talk to them and make sure they are calm and have not panicked. If they are calm and rational, present the end of your canoe for them to grasp. Instruct them not to climb aboard immediately.

If the victims have panicked and are not rational, do not let them grab your canoe. Throw a flotation device to them. Throw it so that it makes contact with them and they can grab it. Once the victims have some support, they should calm down. Then present the end of your canoe as described above.

The Eskimo rescue is a technique you should be aware of if you are paddling with a group of decked craft, such as kayaks. This technique makes it possible for a person in a kayak, by using the end of another craft for support, to reright the craft after it has capsized. (The technique is described more fully in Chapter 4, page 4.34). A kayaker who expects assistance in the form of the Eskimo rescue after a capsizing will beat on the bottom of his boat to attract attention. The kayaker will stay in the boat and move his arms back and forth along the sides of the kayak, feeling for an assisting boat. As soon as you notice that the kayak is upside down, you should quickly present the end of your boat for the kayaker to grab.

The canoe-over-canoe is used most often when

a capsizing occurs some distance from shore. It is simply a matter of getting the submerged canoe across the gunwales of your craft, as shown (Fig. 3–42). Do this by carefully lifting one end of the submerged canoe, rolling it over to an upside-down position, and then as carefully bringing it across the gunwales of your canoe. At this point the canoe is emptied of water, rolled upright, and slid back into the water. The paddlers re-enter their "saved" canoe as you brace the boats together side by side for greater stability, and their rescue is complete. During this rescue have the victims hang on to the ends of your canoe. Talk to them, re-assure them, and tell them what to do. This technique is used on slow-moving sections of deep rivers with much success.

The end-tank dump is an alternative to the canoe-over-canoe rescue. This maneuver is often useful when speed is essential and you have the balance and strength to perform it without risking your own upset (Fig. 3–43). As in the canoe-over-canoe, have the victims hang on to the ends of your canoe and help stabilize it. You grab the end of their canoe and get it up on the gunwale of your canoe. Then turn it upside down and lift it high over your head, with the other end floating on its end-tank flotation. Quickly turn the canoe rightside up and set it back down on the water. The victims can then re-enter, using the method described in canoe-over-canoe rescue. This technique is not for everyone, as it requires a fair amount of strength and balance to execute it properly. It also requires end flotation gear in the canoe.

Fig. 3–42
The canoe-over-canoe rescue

3.57

Fig. 3–43
The end-tank dump as done on shore. From this position, quickly turn canoe upright and set it on the water. This maneuver can also be performed from a canoe.

Chapter 4
Fundamentals of Kayaking

This chapter will present to the beginning kayaker the skill and knowledge necessary for enjoyable, safe kayak paddling on flat water. Such water encompasses lakes, bays, ponds, and other types of impoundments that do not have noticeable currents. Canals and wide, deep rivers can be used for practice, but the surface of the water must be flat. Chapters 4 and 6 cover the paddling of kayaks on rivers with currents in excess of 1 mile per hour. Be sure that you have read Chapter 1 before you read any further.

EQUIPMENT
The Kayak

The modern kayak is a unique craft. Its light-weight construction is well-suited to flat-water touring. There is an increasing interest in this pastime, and the styles of kayaks now available reflect this interest. This chapter will deal primarily with K-1's (one-person kayaks) and how to paddle them.

An excellent kayak to learn in is shown in Chapter 1, Figure 1–4. The plastic construction and hull design, with moderate rocker, are important because they contribute to ease of handling and paddling. The kayak should be equipped with a seat, foot braces, knee braces, flotation bags, a spray skirt, and end loops.

Foot and Knee Braces

Braces should be adjustable, so that you will have a firm fit while seated in your boat. Avoid the use of rigid bar-foot braces because they can trap the feet. The pedestal type or a breakaway bar type is commonly used. Knee braces are used in conjunction with foot braces and are not adjustable. There should be no rough edges anywhere, inside or out, that may cut or injure you.

Flotation Bags

Such flotation gear is a must in your kayak. The bags displace water when you capsize, thereby saving you much time and effort in emptying your craft. Also, your kayak will not otherwise

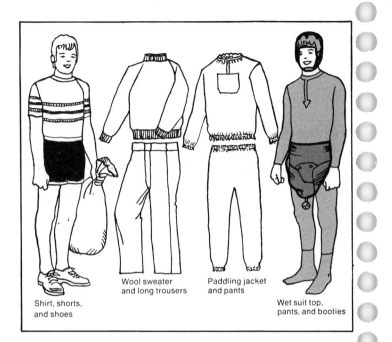

Shirt, shorts, and shoes

Wool sweater and long trousers

Paddling jacket and pants

Wet suit top, pants, and booties

Fig. 4–1
Layers of clothing

float when filled with water. As a beginner you will practice getting out of the kayak from a capsized situation. Also, while practicing the Eskimo rescue and Eskimo roll, you will have some unsuccessful attempts, from which you will have to rescue your capsized kayak.

Spray Skirt

The spray skirt attaches to the coaming around the cockpit and is designed to keep water out of the kayak. It should fit snugly around your body by means of an elastic top. The bottom of the skirt fits snugly around the coaming in the same manner. All spray skirts should have a release loop at the front. This loop must be exposed whenever the skirt is in place. A slight pull forward and up on the loop will release the spray skirt easily from the coaming should a wet exit be necessary (see Chapter 1).

Grab Loops

Grab loops are essential for self-rescue because they offer a firm grip on an otherwise slippery boat. They are also used in securing the kayak for transporting.

Sponges

A sponge is a useful item to have tied inside your kayak. It is very useful in getting small but annoying amounts of water out of your kayak without your having to get out. Because of the small cockpit there is not enough room to use a bailer.

Life Jackets

It is important that the life jacket you use not bind in the midsection of your body when you bend forward from a seated position. Such binding often results in either or both of the following: (1) the life jacket rides up on you; (2) it creates an uncomfortable restriction of movement. Many excellent life jackets are either cut a little shorter or you are able to fold up the bottom 4 to 6 inches so that the device does not interfere with your position.

Helmets

A helmet is necessary because you will need to remain in the kayak when it capsizes so that you can right it, and there is the possibility of striking your head on an underwater obstruction.

Any head protection is better than none, but if you have a choice get a whitewater helmet. This helmet is designed specifically with the paddler in mind. As you can see (Fig. 4–1), it is vented and can be securely fastened. It is also of lightweight but sturdy construction and impervious to water damage.

The Paddle

The basic means of propulsion for the kayak is the double-bladed paddle. You should search out and use a paddle with feathered blades. This paddle has either spoon or flat blades, which are offset 90 degrees from each other (see Chapter 3, Fig. 3–5). With the advent of feathered paddles (offset blades), the feathering of the blade on the recovery is accomplished automatically, as the opposite blade is used for propulsion. If an unfeathered paddle is used, the recovering blade will push against the air, a disadvantage on a windy day.

Slalom paddles range in length from 80 to 85 inches. If you are about 5 feet 9 inches tall, your paddle should be about 82½ inches long.

When selecting a paddle, be sure you understand the meaning of left- and right-hand control (see Blade Control, page 4.7). Also, get a one-piece paddle, since two-part jointed paddles are not as sturdy as the one-piece paddle. For the beginner, flat-bladed paddles are preferred, as they will be easier to master and can be used for either left or right control.

CLOTHING

Clothing is very much a personal matter. When you select clothing for kayaking, however, pay particular attention to its insulating properties (wet or dry) and its tendency to restrict your movements. Long pants are worn by some kayakers even in mild or warm weather to protect their legs from rough spots in the boat (see Fig. 4–1).

Paddle Jackets

A paddle jacket is very useful in kayaking. It is a lightweight, waterproof jacket with adjustable closures at the waist, cuffs, and collar that will help protect you from the effects of cold water and wind chill. In colder conditions the jacket can be paired with pants of the same material. Remember that your comfort is the key to your ability both to learn and to paddle effectively.

Shoes

It is important to wear shoes in a kayak. Many kayaks are built of fiber glass and consequently may have rough inner surfaces or even small burrs that can cut unprotected feet. Also, you must think ahead to the time when you might have to walk or portage some distance. A good pair of shoes (water tolerant) are a blessing. Low-top tennis shoes seem to be the best all-round choice.

LAUNCHING AND BOARDING

It will be readily apparent that the kayak is easily carried by one person (see Chaper 1, Fig. 1–11). If, however, you find yourself in a situation where a person is obviously overburdened, offer assistance.

It is best to launch a kayak parallel to shore or the edge of a dock. The basics of launching and boarding have already been discussed in Chapter 1, pages 1.12–18.

Trim and Balance

Since the cockpit and seat are permanently installed in most kayaks, the only factor affecting the trim of the kayak is the storage of duffel. The rule of thumb is to trim the kayak level, or slightly stern heavy. The placement of duffel can be facilitated by the partial deflating of the flotation bags or by the use of undersized bags.

Many touring kayaks are designed with built-in storage compartments. As always, distribute the weight to keep the kayak level from side to side and from bow to stern.

Stability

Once aboard your kayak, and while still in shallow water close to shore, make sure you have the "feel" of your boat. Try rocking it from side to side, and make sure you fit comfortably but firmly in the kayak. If you have not yet practiced a wet exit (see Chapter 1), do so before you work on the various strokes and maneuvers.

EFFECTIVE PADDLING

The simplicity of the strokes you need to know will become apparent to you as you experiment with them. It will be more difficult, however, to achieve the finesse needed to perform these strokes efficiently. The strokes themselves have a great deal in common.

Hand Position

Proper hand position on the paddle shaft is a matter of preference to experienced paddlers, but the consensus is that you should grasp the shaft as shown (Fig. 4–2).

Please note that the elbows are at 90-degree angles to the paddle shaft, as are the forearms. When paddling you should try to maintain a firm grip on the shaft with your control hand. With

feathered, spoon-shaped blades, the paddle blades are offset 90 degrees.

Fig. 4–2
Grasp the kayak paddle so that elbows are at 90-degree angles.

Blade Control

In Figure 3–5, Chapter 3, paddle D is right-hand control, paddle C is left-hand control. Of these spoon-bladed paddles, right control is by far the most commonly used. Paddle A has flat blades and can be used with either left- or right-hand control. A paddle is "left control" if as you make a forward stroke on the left the power face of the right blade is facing up. If the power face of the right blade is facing down, you have a "right-control" paddle. Flat-bladed paddles can be used either way because any face of the blade can be the power face. The control hand always maintains a firm grip on the shaft and controls the rotating of the paddle from stroke to stroke. The other hand permits the shaft to rotate within its grasp between strokes but maintains a firm grasp during strokes. This paddle rotation is explained in detail on page 4.9.

Ideally, you should move the kayak through the water, not the paddle. For instance, in the forward stroke, once the paddle is inserted in the water, the kayak is drawn ahead to the paddle rather than the paddle being pulled to you.

All strokes fall into one of two categories: those in which you "pull" on the water and those in which you "push" on the water. The face of the blade that pulls on the water is called the power face. The face of the blade that pushes on the water is called the back face. Examples of strokes that pull on the water with the power face are the forward stroke, the forward sweep, the draw, and the high brace. Strokes that push on the water with the back face include the backstroke, the reverse sweep, and the low brace. With spoon-bladed paddles, the inside of the curved blade is the power face.

Once the kayak is moving, it is relatively easy to keep it doing so, as opposed to stopping and starting again. Also, with the slalom kayak, once you have forward momentum and stop paddling, the kayak will have a tendency to skew to one side or the other, rather than continuing on a straight course.

The combining of strokes in kayaking to gain a
desired reaction of the boat is not done to the same
degree that it is in canoeing. This is so because the
double-bladed paddle offers control on both sides
of the kayak.

Fluency in kayaking, however, depends greatly
on your ability to use strokes not just to propel and
turn, but to "brace" as well. Greater power and
efficiency result when your entire body is used in
maneuvering the kayak, not just the arms. Such
maneuvering can be accomplished with minimal
risk of capsizing if your strokes do two things at
once: propel or turn the kayak and support part of
your body weight. Thus, every stroke involves not
just moving the paddle through the water, but
using your entire body to move the kayak. This
bracing part of a stroke can be added if you use
the blade at an angle to the water surface, but not
perpendicular to it. Such an angle is referred to as
a climbing angle (Fig. 4–3).

When the blade is at a climbing angle and
moved through the water, it tries to rise up, or

Fig. 4–3
*"Climbing angle" of the blade, for support
during a forward sweep*

climb, to the surface of the water. The more power applied to moving the blade through the water, the more weight the blade can support.

As you become more at ease in the kayak and more familiar with the basic strokes, your instructor will have you modify almost all your strokes to include a climbing angle. In this manner you may use your body strength rather than just arm strength. Thus, your strokes and maneuvers will become more efficient and less tiring.

Paddle Rotation

For a right-control paddle, for the first stroke on the right side, the right blade should be vertical as it enters the water forward of you, with the shaft about 45 degrees diagonally in front of you. Grasp the shaft firmly with each hand as you pull the paddle along the right side of the kayak with your right arm as the left hand punches forward from near your head. At the end of the stroke, lift the right blade out of the water, ease your grasp on the left, and let the shaft rotate within your left hand

as the right hand rotates its knuckles up until the left blade is vertical, power face facing astern. Again the paddle will be about 45 degrees diagonally in front of your body. As the left blade enters the water, the left hand firmly grasps the shaft for the stroke on the left. For the next stroke on the right, rotate the paddle back to the original position in the same manner. The rotation of the paddle between strokes should be executed crisply and cleanly. It will take a little practice to get used to, but it will soon become automatic.

Be sure to practice this technique on shore before you first attempt to paddle in the kayak. For a left-control paddle, everything would be the same except that the left hand is the control hand and will always maintain a firm grasp on the shaft as the right hand permits the shaft to rotate within its grasp.

Strokes

The primary strokes for paddling a kayak are described below, augmented with a series of illustrations. For the sake of brevity, the strokes are described as being done on one side. However, all of the strokes dealt with here must be mastered on both sides.

In the following stroke descriptions the term "lower arm" refers to the hand and arm that are grasping the paddle shaft on the side on which the stroke is being taken. For example, when a stroke is taken on the right side, the right arm is the lower arm. The term "top arm" refers to the hand and arm away from the side on which the stroke is being taken. The names of most strokes are descriptive of the stroke.

STROKES

The Forward Stroke

Purpose. To move the kayak forward.

Description. The blade enters the water perpendicular to the keel line comfortably forward of the paddler. The lower arm is extended forward as the top arm is cocked with its hand near the head. The shoulder of the lower arm is rotated slightly forward.

The paddle pulls with the power face along the side of the kayak parallel to the keel line. The top arm punches forward as the lower arm pulls, with the shoulders rotating to add body power to the stroke. Two-thirds of the power is "pull" and one-third is "push."

The top arm is fully extended in front of the body, and the lower arm is bent alongside the body as the stroke ends. Recovery is made by means of slicing the blade cleanly out of the water and quickly rotating the opposite blade into position for its stroke. Feathering of the blade is automatic with offset blades, as the next stroke is done on the opposite side.

Synopsis. The bow will tend to turn away from the paddling side as the boat moves forward. Repeated strokes on alternating sides of the kayak will result in the kayak's moving straight ahead. Repeated strokes on only one side will result in the bow's turning away from the stroke in a circle as the kayak moves forward (Fig. 4–4).

Fig. 4-4
The forward stroke

4.13

The Backstroke

Purpose. To move the kayak backward or to stop forward motion.

Description. The blade enters the water alongside the kayak just behind the paddler. The blade is perpendicular to the keel line. The lower arm is bent, with its elbow over the shaft. The top arm is extended forward, with its hand out over the water. The shoulders are rotated toward the paddling side.

The paddle pushes with the back face along the side of the kayak parallel to the keel line. Power is applied with the top arm and its shoulder pulling up and back as the lower arm pushes down and forward. The shoulders rotate to add body strength to the stroke.

The stroke ends as the lower arm is extended forward and the top arm is bent and near the head. The blade is sliced from the water, a comfortable distance forward of the paddler, and the paddle is rotated into position for the stroke on the opposite side. The blade is feathered and recovered automatically as the same stroke is taken on the opposite side.

Synopsis. The bow will tend to turn toward the paddling side as the kayak moves backward. With repeated strokes on alternating sides, the kayak will tend to travel backward in a straight line. Repeated strokes on only one side will result in the kayak's turning in a circle, bow toward the paddle side, as the kayak moves backward (Fig. 4–5).

Fig. 4–5
The backstroke

The Forward Sweep

Purpose. To turn the bow away from the paddling side while the kayak moves forward.

Description. The blade enters the water next to the bow, well forward of the paddler, with the blade vertical to the water surface. The lower arm is extended forward and its shoulder rotated forward, with the body leaning forward as well. The top arm is cocked, with the hand near the shoulder.

With the shaft relatively low, the blade is pulled out from the bow and through a large arc to the stern of the kayak. Power is applied to the power face with the lower arm and shoulder pulling as the top arm and shoulder push forward. The shoulders should rotate at least 90 degrees during the stroke.

The stroke ends near the stern, with the lower arm extended toward the stern as the top arm is extended forward and across the body. The paddle could be rotated into position for a forward sweep on the opposite side, but it is highly unlikely that such a stroke would be done. It would often be desirable to take another forward sweep on the same side, in which case the blade would be feathered and swung through an arc for another stroke starting near the bow.

Synopsis. The bow of the kayak will swing quickly away from the paddling side as the kayak moves forward. Repeated strokes will result in a very tight turn with very little headway. Three good sweeps should spin the kayak 360 degrees (Fig. 4–6).

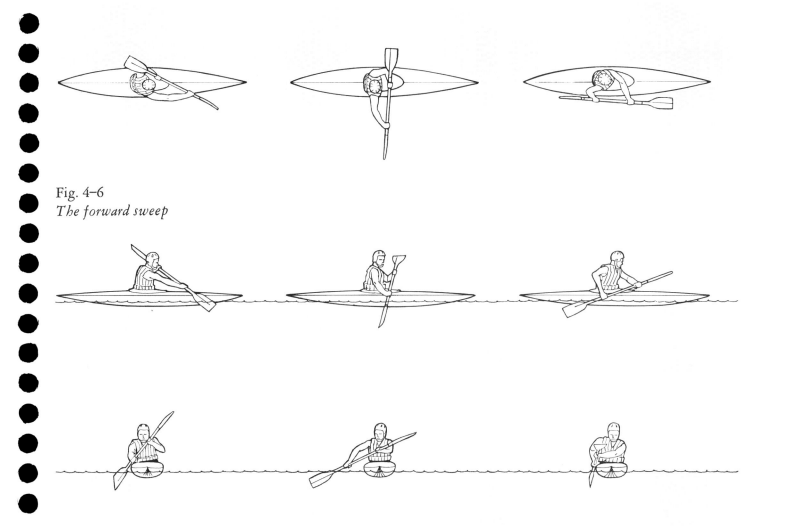

Fig. 4–6
The forward sweep

The Reverse Sweep

Purpose. To sharply turn the bow toward the paddling side while headway is reduced.

Description. The blade enters the water, vertically, well astern of the paddler. The paddler's body is rotated toward the paddling side, with the lower arm extended toward the stern, elbow slightly bent, and the top arm extended low and out over the water.

The blade is pushed out from the stern, with the back face, and forward toward the bow in a large arc. Power is applied with the lower arm pushing out from the stern as the body and shoulders rotate and the top arm pulls the shaft in front of the body just above the cockpit.

The stroke ends near the bow with the body leaning slightly forward. The blade is lifted from the water and feathered in an arc back to the stern for another stroke. It is not likely that a reverse sweep would be done on the other side at this time.

Synopsis. The bow will turn sharply toward the paddling side and move slightly backward. Repeated strokes on the same side will pivot the kayak 360 degrees (about three good strokes), with very little sternway. A reverse sweep if performed while the kayak has headway will stop the kayak, as well as turn it (Fig. 4–7).

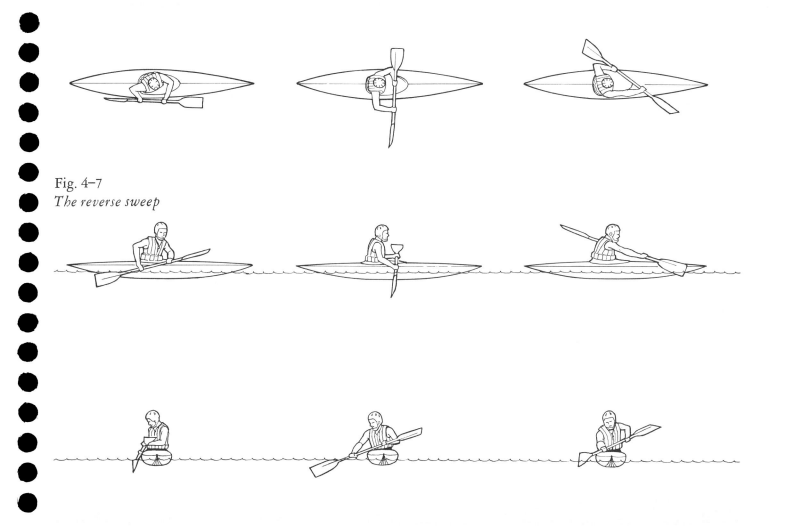

Fig. 4–7
The reverse sweep

The Drawstroke

Purpose. To move the kayak sideways toward the paddling side.

Description. The blade enters the water a comfortable distance to the side of the paddler, parallel to the keel line. The lower arm is extended, with the top arm cocked over the head.

Power is applied with the top arm punching out from over the head as the lower arm pulls the blade toward the paddler's side perpendicular to the keel line.

The stroke ends as recovery begins about 6 inches from the side. To recover, you can rotate the blade 90 degrees (power face aft) and slice through the water to begin another draw; or you can slice the blade from the water toward the stern by lowering your top arm toward the bow and then swinging the feathered blade in an arc to start another stroke. Do not let the boat run into the paddle.

Synopsis. The boat will move directly sideways to the paddling side without turning or moving forward or backward (Fig. 4–8).

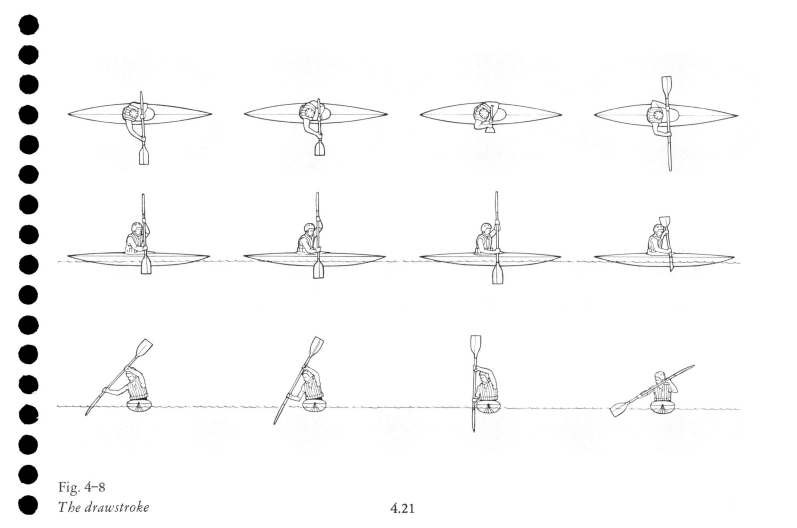

Fig. 4–8
The drawstroke

4.21

The High Brace

Purpose. To aid in maintaining stability.

Description. As the kayak begins to lean or capsize toward the paddle side, reach straight out to the side with the blade, as in the drawstroke, but keep the paddle shaft nearly horizontal rather than vertical. Generally, the top arm will be cocked and near the head as the lower arm is extended.

Power is applied with the lower arm and upper body pulling down on the power face as the knees and hips sharply bring the kayak back to a level position under the body.

The stroke ends as the kayak and paddler regain stability. The paddle blade should not move very much. To recover, the blade is sliced out of the water and swung in an arc to the start of another stroke.

Synopsis. The boat will stabilize in a level position and move slightly sideways toward the paddle side, or if it is bracing on moving water, it will stabilize in a leaned position for a prolonged period (Fig. 4–9).

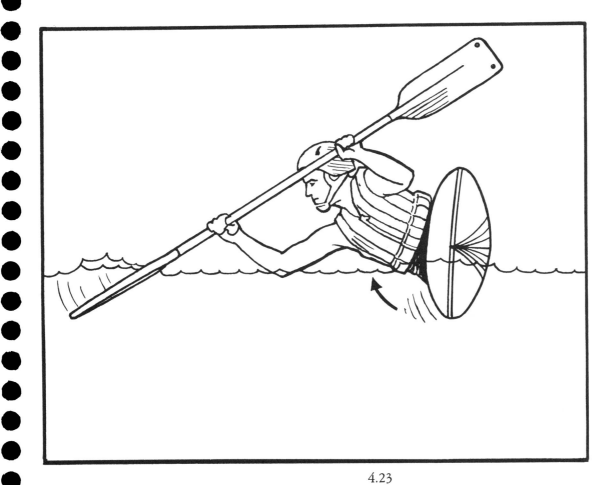

Fig. 4–9
The high brace uses the power face of the blade.

The Low Brace

Purpose. To powerfully return the kayak and paddler to a stable position.

Description. The blade enters the water out to the side or slightly astern of the paddler's position. The lower arm is bent, with its elbow directly over the shaft. The top arm is bent and immediately in front of the body.

Power is applied directly downward on the back face, with the lower arm pushing as the hips and knees sharply pull the kayak into a level and stable position. The top arm pulls upward slightly or remains in place.

The stroke ends as the kayak becomes stable. To recover, slice the blade out of the water and swing in an arc, feathered, to begin another stroke.

Synopsis. The boat will regain a stable position, or in moving water, become stable at a given lean. The low brace is usually done as a last-second attempt to prevent an upset (Fig. 4–10).

Fig. 4–10
The low brace uses the back face of the blade.

Maneuvers

Maneuvering a kayak requires practice and a firm understanding of all the basic strokes. So far, only pure strokes have been presented, but you will need to develop the ability to combine two or more of these into one smooth action. In this way you will be able to execute specific maneuvers with precision control.

Also useful is an understanding of the turning circle. Strokes that follow a path along the turning circle are, generally, the most efficient in turning the kayak. As you do a forward sweep, the blade of the paddle is traveling along a part of the turning circle, an imaginary circle passing through each end of the craft and centered at you its pivot point.

The Pivot Turn

You can pivot your kayak in place by using a good forward sweep on one side and a reverse sweep on the other. In each case your strokes are along the turning circle. To put more power into this maneuver, you must put more of your body into these strokes. You can lean your body out and be supported by your strokes if you add a bracing component with the blade. This maneuver is accomplished by means of changing the blade angle in the water from vertical to a climbing angle, as mentioned earlier (Fig. 4–11).

Practice. To make sure you are pivoting in place and not going forward or backward in a small circle, place a buoy next to you and try to keep it alongside the cockpit during the turn, or set out a circle of buoys to turn within. Try different strokes or combinations and see how your kayak responds. Use repeated forward sweeps or reverse sweeps, or use a forward sweep on one side, then a reverse sweep on the opposite side. What is the fewest number of strokes you can use to turn 360 degrees? Does the kayak stay in place or move forward or back some as it turns?

Sideslipping

You can move a kayak sideways if you use draw-strokes on the desired side. However, when you

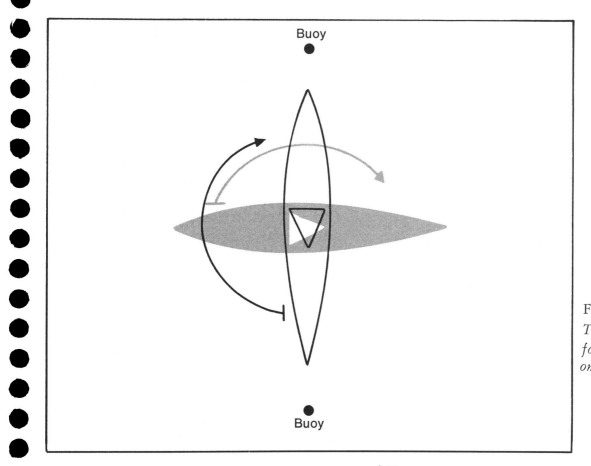

Fig. 4–11
The pivot turn. Alternate forward and reverse sweeps on opposite sides.

move forward through the water, it is generally better to use stationary draws.

A stationary draw is essentially the same as a draw except that—

- The leading edge of the blade is angled away from the keel line at 30 to 45 degrees.
- The paddle is held in place with the blade fully immersed in the water.

A stationary draw utilizes the movement of the kayak through the water as the blade is held in a fixed position relative to the boat. As the boat ceases to move, the stroke ceases to function, and power strokes must then be used.

It will take a little practice to learn exactly where to put the stroke to maintain your heading. If the stroke is too far forward, the bow will swing to the paddle side. If it is too far aft, the stern will swing to the paddle side.

Practice. You should use an anchored buoy or other obstacle to sideslip past. To practice draws under control, use the edge of a dock or the shoreline as a reference (Fig. 4–12).

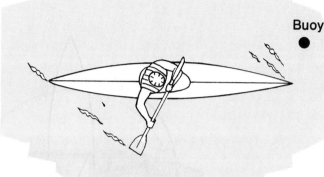

Fig. 4–12
Sideslipping with a stationary draw

The Duffek

The Duffek is a combination of strokes for crisply turning your moving kayak and maintaining forward momentum. It combines the stationary draw, the high brace, the draw, and forward strokes in one fluid motion. Start with your kayak moving forward briskly and use a stationary draw out from the side of the kayak forward of your body.

As the kayak slows, draw toward the bow and then go smoothly into a forward stroke. This should turn your kayak at least 90 degrees. As you practice and become at ease with this combination, you can then start to lean onto the stroke more and more during the high brace and draw portions (Fig. 4–13).

Some useful drills. Such drills include making the turn around a buoy or around the corner of a dock. See if you can make a 180-degree turn with a single Duffek.

Paddling a Straight Line

Slalom kayaks, like the one you may be using, will not continue on a straight course, so it is necessary to make constant but slight variations in the forward stroke to maintain a straight course. Usually these variations will be in the form of paddling a little "wide" (almost a sweep), or of varying the amount of power applied to each stroke. Sight over the bow at a destination and as soon as the slightest turn begins, make a correction for it.

Do not wait until the boat is 45 degrees off course or you will end up stopping to get pointed in the right direction again. Practice until it feels natural and automatic to go straight. With practice you will learn to anticipate the boat's actions.

Practice. To develop an awareness of the boat's tendency to turn and to practice the variations of the forward stroke that are needed to prevent this turning, try paddling your kayak along a straight object for a moderate distance. A shoreline, dock, poolside, or buoyed rope will do. Keep your boat on course parallel to the object and gradually, as you develop better control, paddle closer to the object. This exercise can be practiced both forward and backward.

Gates

A series of gates (two suspended poles or anchored buoys make one gate) are useful in assisting your development of precision control. An English gate is one gate with a set sequence of maneuvers (see Chapter 3, Fig. 3–37). Or a series of three or four gates provides versatility and lets

Fig. 4–13

*The Duffek combines the stationary draw,
high brace, draw, and forward strokes.*

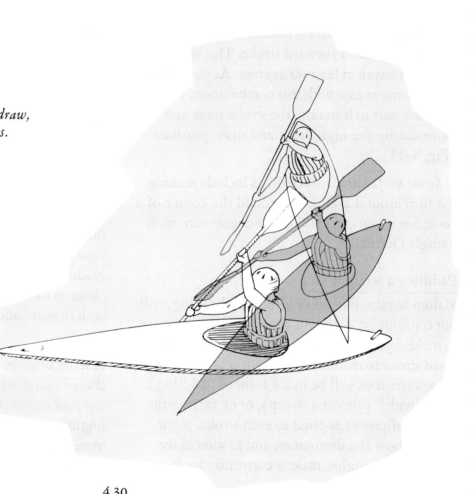

you design your own course, for a constantly changing challenge to your skills. Remember, anything that can be done forward can be done backward as well.

A description of several paddling drills for canoeists appears in Chapter 3, starting on page 3.43. These drills work equally well for kayakers.

RESCUE

Your instruction in paddling is incomplete until you have learned how to handle yourself and your boat when mishaps occur. The most frequent mishap in a kayak is capsizing. Your best defense is a good Eskimo roll or Eskimo rescue. You should also be familiar with techniques to assist others.

Self-Rescue:
From the Eskimo Rescue to the Eskimo Roll

The Eskimo roll is your most important method of self-rescue in kayaking. Should you capsize you have two choices: (1) do a wet exit and swim the kayak to shore; or (2) stay in the boat and roll back up using the Eskimo rescue or the Eskimo roll. Needless to say, staying in your kayak is preferred.

To practice the Eskimo roll you will need a properly fitted kayak, a spray skirt, a helmet, a life jacket, a swimsuit, and shoes. A paddle jacket and other clothing may be useful if you are practicing outdoors. Some people find nose clips useful also. You will need a paddle, but not for the initial steps. Most important of all, you will need an experienced instructor to aid you in correcting your errors. Get into a rolling session sponsored by a local canoe or kayak club where quality help abounds.

The following sequence is presented in a progression of steps leading to the Eskimo roll. Other valuable self-rescue skills are part of the learning sequence, including the Eskimo rescue and the paddle brace recovery. This learning sequence is needed to acquire the timing, flexibility, and coordination that you must master to successfully perform the Eskimo roll. You will find it helpful to read this entire section a couple of times before you begin to concentrate on any one step. (Be sure to practice wet exits first, page 1.20.)

The key component of an Eskimo roll is commonly called the hip snap. Although it really takes the whole body to accomplish this move, it is the action of the hips that rotates the kayak upright from its capsized position, with you still in it.

During the key phase of a roll, your upper torso is extended out to the side of the boat near the surface. Your upper torso stays in this relative position as your lower body (hips and knees) forcefully snaps the kayak upright from the capsized position.

The other components of the roll are the set-up (getting your paddle and body into position to come up with the hip snap) and the recovery (bracing to bring your body over the kayak in a stable position after the kayak is upright). These components will be covered in steps 5, 6, and 7 below.

Step 1. This first step is a poolside drill. You will use the side of the pool as a support to help you roll upright after capsizing. Simply grasp the pool deck or gutter and capsize to that side. Use your hips and knees to press the boat upright in a snappy manner, keeping your head at water level. Try these drills on both sides. It will be useful later on to be able to roll on either side. If a pool is not available, you may have an assistant hold a paddle at water level for you to grasp, or the bow of another boat.

Practice until the action feels smooth, natural, and relaxed. It should not require a great deal of force on your hands and arms. Notice that in Figure 4–14 the paddler's head comes up last as the paddler's upper body is brought out of the water and back over the kayak. Remember, the hips do the work, not the arms.

Step 2. In the second step you capsize to one side and recover to the opposite side. You do this by capsizing to the right, for example, and reaching for a paddle shaft held by your partner on the left. The side of the pool or other support could be

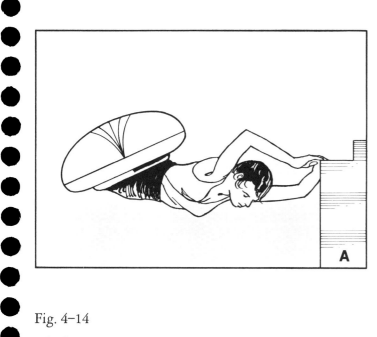

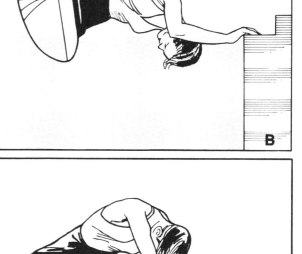

Fig. 4–14

The hip snap. It is important to bring the head up last.

used just as well. From here, do a hip snap up, as in step 1.

Remember, your head and shoulders must come out of the water last. If your head and shoulders come up too soon, you will find yourself relying heavily on your hands and arms to complete the roll up. Your partner will be able to tell you how much force you are applying.

Once you and your partner agree that you are applying minimal force with your hands and that you have a good hip snap, you are ready for step 3.

Step 3. In the third step you hold your partner's fingertips or interlock one finger of each hand with the same fingers of your partner's and capsize toward him. Remembering to apply 90 percent of your effort to your hip- and knee-braces, force the kayak to slide under you in one motion. If you have been overdependent on the force applied by your hands in rolling up, it will really show up here. You may have to revert to step 2 for more practice before advancing to this step. The

ultimate test in step 3 is to accomplish repeated attempts to either side by interlocking little fingers with your partner.

Step 4. The Eskimo rescue necessitates the use of a stable support, such as the end of another kayak. Essentially what should happen is that once you are upside down, another kayak should quickly come to your aid. Do not wet exit; instead, hold your breath, get your hands out of the water so that you can pound on your boat to get attention, and then move your arms forward and back to feel for an assisting boat. Be ready to grasp the bow of the assisting kayak (Fig. 4–15).

After you grasp the bow, a snap of the hips and a slight push down on the bow of the assisting kayak will bring you up. With the proper timing, you will find that this assisted-rescue skill is as easy as it sounds.

When you first practice the Eskimo rescue, start by holding on to the bow of another kayak and deliberately capsizing. Then use the bow of the

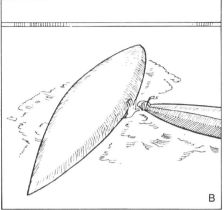

Fig. 4–15

The Eskimo rescue. Pound on the hull to attract attention, then feel for another boat. Use the end of the rescuing boat for support to right yourself.

assisting kayak as support to roll upright, as in step 1.

Practice with a purpose. While practicing the Eskimo rescue, keep in mind that your ultimate goal is the Eskimo roll to either side. The Eskimo rescue is only one step toward that goal. Remember that your ability to perform this simple rescue requires assistance from others in your group. You need to practice righting yourself as well as assisting others. Other paddlers need to be aware of their vital role in the Eskimo rescue.

Step 5. You finally use the kayak paddle to prevent your capsizing by doing a paddle brace recovery. You should be quite familiar by now with just how far you can lean before capsizing. In this drill, get close to shore and put one blade on shore.

Lean out over the water to the point of capsizing, then a little farther. As you begin to capsize, apply pressure down on the paddle to right yourself. Do this several times, leaning out farther and farther each time. Continue until you are able to recover from about 90 degrees; remember the hip snap. This skill is much like the drawstroke mentioned earlier in this chapter. Now you are ready for the real brace. Instead of reaching directly to the side, reach ahead of your position and to the side of the bow.

With your partner standing by, begin to lean out to the critical point of capsizing. Just as you begin to capsize, press the face of the paddle against the surface of the water and sweep it across the surface at a climbing angle, applying a downward force on the blade.

This action should bring you upright again by the time the blade is directly abeam of you. If you are unsuccessful, your partner can assist you with an Eskimo rescue. Continue to practice, leaning out farther each time. Many paddlers can go over far enough to drink the water and still recover. You might try a draw at the end of the sweep to help you recover.

Step 6. This step consists of a half roll. All the elements for the roll are here. You will capsize to

4.36

one side, perform the brace learned in the last step, use a good hip snap, and roll back up on the same side.

As you see in Figure 4–16A, you will be holding one blade in your top hand, with the other blade flat to the water. This "extended-paddle grip" serves two purposes: (1) it provides more effective support for the paddle; and (2) it helps you control the blade angle.

With the power face up, swing the paddle across the deck of the kayak to the set-up position. Lean forward and capsize away from the paddle.

Now that you are upside down, the paddle blade is properly placed for the application of the paddle brace (Fig. 4–16B). Sweep the blade in a 90-degree circle away from the bow, just as you did in the paddle brace recovery. A properly executed hip snap as you sweep the paddle should bring you up, thus completing the half roll. You may need the assistance of the high brace to complete the roll.

The primary problem encountered in this ma-neuver, other than a poor hip snap, is a loss of blade angle during the sweep. The paddle must skim across the surface with its leading edge slightly raised, at a climbing angle. Wear a diving mask, so that you can watch the blade during the sweep. The mask also aids in keeping water out of your nose until you learn to exhale properly through the nose, which keeps water out.

In addition, your helper can position himself at the blade to guide the blade through the arc and offer some support, initially, to the blade as you apply the paddle brace.

As you become more proficient at the half roll, switch to the other side and hold the paddle in a normal grip, rather than an extended one.

Step 7. Once the half roll is perfected, you will find the transition to the Eskimo roll quite easy and natural. Set up for the roll as in step 6, but capsize toward the paddle, for a full 360-degree roll.

The Eskimo roll is described fully with the assistance of the diagrams shown in Figure 4–17.

Fig. 4–16A

The set-up position for the Eskimo roll. The extended-paddle grip will provide more effective support during the Eskimo roll.

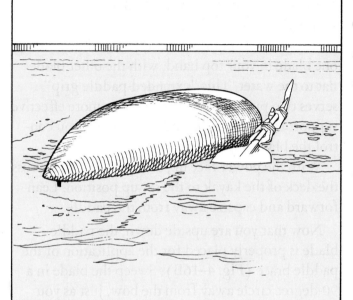

Fig. 4–16B

Capsized in the set-up position (seen from the bow)

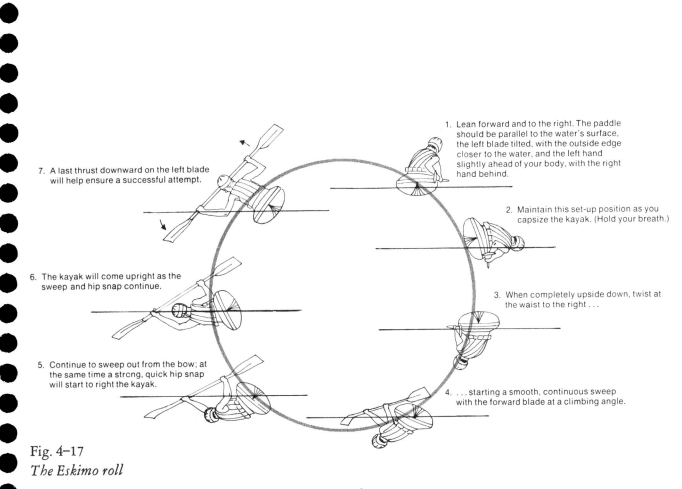

1. Lean forward and to the right. The paddle should be parallel to the water's surface, the left blade tilted, with the outside edge closer to the water, and the left hand slightly ahead of your body, with the right hand behind.

2. Maintain this set-up position as you capsize the kayak. (Hold your breath.)

3. When completely upside down, twist at the waist to the right . . .

4. . . . starting a smooth, continuous sweep with the forward blade at a climbing angle.

5. Continue to sweep out from the bow; at the same time a strong, quick hip snap will start to right the kayak.

6. The kayak will come upright as the sweep and hip snap continue.

7. A last thrust downward on the left blade will help ensure a successful attempt.

Fig. 4–17
The Eskimo roll

Rescue of Others

In addition to taking care of yourself, you should be able to lend assistance to others in need.

Towing

On a lake or similar body of water, when a paddler has capsized and then exited from the kayak, you can tow him and his boat to shore by presenting your stern to him so that he can hold on to your grab loop. It will take some strength and time to tow a paddler and his kayak to shore (Fig. 4–18).

Fig. 4–18   *A towing assist*

The Kayak-Over-Kayak

If the victim is a long distance from shore, and especially if the water is cold, you should try to empty the kayak of water and help him to re-enter it in deep water. It is possible to do a kayak-over-kayak rescue that is very similar to the canoe-over-canoe rescue described in Chapter 2. Have the victim hang on to the stern of your kayak as you pull his upside-down kayak up onto your deck. If the victim's kayak has flotation bags to prevent too much water from collecting inside it, you will be able to balance his kayak across yours and rock the water from one end to the other to empty the water out of the cockpit. Once the kayak is empty of water, roll it upright and slide it back into the water (Fig. 4–19).

The Deepwater Re-entry

You can assist a victim to re-enter his kayak in deep water by bracing it alongside yours with the paddles across both boats (Fig. 4–20) and by having him climb on board as you stabilize the boats.

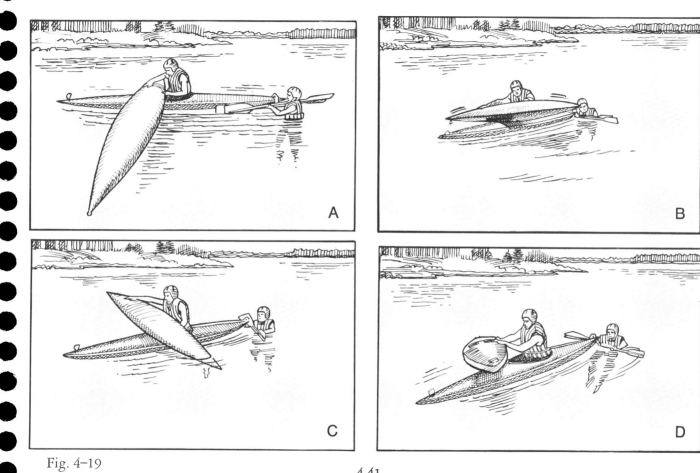

Fig. 4–19
The kayak-over-kayak rescue

4.41

Fig. 4–20
The deepwater re-entry. Use the paddles to brace the kayaks together as the victim enters the kayak.

Another possibility is for the victim to re-enter the capsized kayak and perform an Eskimo roll or an Eskimo rescue (see page 4.31). Some water will still be in the kayak, which will be manageable with some caution. Remember, in cold water it is very important to get victims out of the water before they are robbed of the strength they need to survive.

On a lake or a calm section of river, the above-mentioned techniques will work perfectly well. Whenever there is an obvious current, however, special precautions must be taken, and speed is essential. Refer to Chapter 7, "Basic River Kayaking," for the techniques that are necessary in this situation.

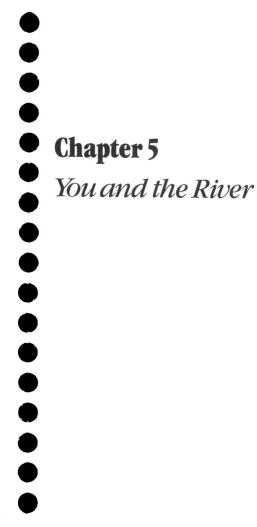

Chapter 5

You and the River

Once you decide to try paddling on rivers or streams, you need to be aware of the very great differences between the waters of a lake and those of a river. The things that may happen to a canoe on a lake are very different from the things that may happen to it on a river. You will need to learn about the special hazards that are peculiar to a river, as well as to acquire the skills, strategies, and knowledge necessary for a safe river outing.

THE POWER OF MOVING WATER

First of all, you should be aware of—and respect— the power of moving water. Drifting along in a 5-mile-an-hour current may seem very tame, but the potential for serious trouble is always present. As an example, imagine a swamped canoe in such a current being carried broadside against a rock and held fast by the power of the water. The force holding that canoe in place is equal to the area of the canoe in square feet (17 feet x 2 feet) times the water velocity squared (5^2) times the constant 2.8 . . . a force of about 2,400 pounds! Not only is this force great enough to hold the canoe in place, it is enough to start collapsing the canoe around the rock. Similarly, a person trying to stand in this current, if only thigh deep, would have a force of about 100 pounds pushing against his legs.

These facts should convince you that the water can work against you far beyond your ability to resist or fight it. However, with an understanding of how the river currents work, you can make this power work for you and not against you. As you can see, if you are going to paddle on a river, there is much to learn about how to safely utilize the power of moving water.

RIVER CURRENTS

One way to avoid a lot of trouble on a river is to follow along with the main part of the water or, in other words, to follow the main current.

The current, however, is seldom uniform all the way across the riverbed. This is true of both the speed of the current and the volume of water.

Water Velocity

Because of friction against the river bottom and the shore, water velocity is not the same all the way across the river. In a straight channel, velocity would tend to be fastest in midstream at the surface (Fig. 5–1). Because of the difference in

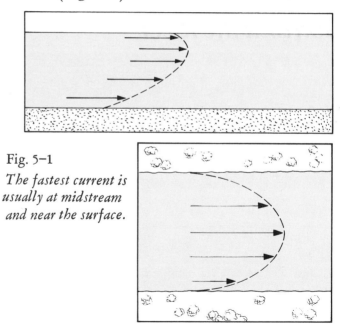

Fig. 5–1
The fastest current is usually at midstream and near the surface.

the speed of the current from the surface to the bottom, a person would not remain in a vertical position, but would be tumbled head first. For this reason, if you should find yourself swimming in the current of the river, keep your hips and feet up at the surface, but also keep your feet downstream as you float on your back. In so doing you will be able to see what is ahead and be able to fend off rocks or other obstructions with your feet.

Water velocity is also affected by the gradient, or slope, of the riverbed. As the gradient becomes steeper, the current flows faster. As a result, the water will also get shallower. Thus the saying, "Still waters run deep." In a slow-moving river where the gradient is minimal, a relatively small volume of water will fill the stream bed. But with the same size riverbed and the same volume of water with a steeper gradient, you will find that the water is shallower. Once you have some experience with a given stream, you will be able to deduce the depth and speed of the river current from changes in the width and gradient of the riverbed. Thus, when the riverbed narrows, you should be able to anticipate that the current will become faster, which usually means a steeper gradient and shallower water. If there is no change in gradient, the water will be deeper.

Bends

Thus far we have been talking about a current flowing parallel to the banks in a straight riverbed. Some interesting things begin to happen when the riverbed turns, or bends. The current, instead of remaining parallel to the shore, continues to flow straight ahead until forced to turn by the outside bank at the bend. When it reaches the outside of the bend, it tends to turn downward and in across the bottom of the river, creating a spiraling flow that leaves room for more surface water on the outside of the bend. The strongest, deepest, and fastest current will be found on the outside of bends. Also, erosion of the outside bank can be fairly rapid, so that trees or shrubs fall into the river because of undercut and eroded banks. For these reasons bends should be approached with caution (Fig. 5–2).

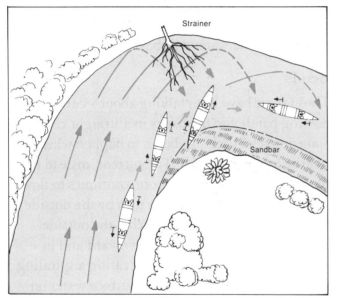

Fig. 5–2

A river bend. Note the current (blue arrows), a strainer, and a safe course.

Along the inside of the bend the current will tend to be slower and shallower. This is the place to be if you are unsure of what lies around the corner. In low water levels you may have to seek the outside of the bend to find water deep enough to float your boat. During periods of high water you should stay near the inside shore to avoid the turbulence of powerful currents and obstacles caused by erosion of the outside bank.

Frequently, just below and on the inside of the bend is an area of calm, still water or an eddy. An eddy is a backward or a circling movement of the water, apart from the main flow. In the case of a river bend, the main current is on the outside of the bend, while from farther downstream a branch of current breaks off and flows to the inside and back upstream. Such an eddy is usually calm and large: an ideal place for a group of boats to gather to rest or reorganize.

Ledges and Gravel Bars

Less obvious features exist that may cause the

current to flow at an angle to the shoreline. Such features include ledges and gravel bars. Because they are often not visible lying beneath the surface of the water, they are difficult to detect in advance.

It is important that you always be aware of the direction of the current that your boat is in, because your boat is going in that direction and not necessarily in the direction in which it is pointed. When there are no obstructions in the river this fact is not so important, but when there are many rocks sticking up in the water around you, you had better know in which direction your boat is traveling. Many a beginner has found his boat stuck on a rock because he did not know the direction of the current. Do not depend on the direction of the bow as an indicator of the direction you are going in. Instead, develop the habit of observing small bits of foam or debris floating on the water nearby. They are very likely going where the current is going. Also, you should develop the habit of sighting references along the shore to indicate your direction. You may also sight an

obstacle ahead of you against the background. If the alignment stays unchanged, you are heading directly for that obstacle. You then need to take immediate action to avoid it. It is best to keep your boat in line with the current and move the whole boat sideways enough to avoid the obstacle, rather than turning the canoe and trying to paddle around it (Fig. 5-3).

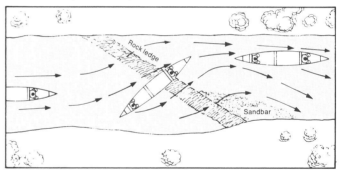

Fig. 5-3

Diagonal currents at ledges or gravel bars.
Keep your canoe parallel to the current.

By keeping the boat parallel to the current, you present only the width of your boat to an obstacle;

thus, to avoid hitting it you need move the boat only its own width. If, on the other hand, you turn your boat, you must then move it its length to avoid a collision.

Ledges and gravel bars frequently cause the river to divide into two or more channels. Some sections of the river may be blocked by exposed parts of the ledge or bar. These can easily be seen and avoided, but many other places may be too shallow to float your canoe. It may be difficult to locate a deep channel that you can navigate. Frequently your only clue is a subtle change in the color of the water. A darker hue usually indicates the deeper water. Sometimes at a gravel bar there is no clear channel. If you find yourself running aground in the shallows associated with a bar, you should step out of the boat and walk into deeper waters before you re-enter and paddle on.

Chutes

You should notice that ledges usually present a broad obstacle in that the ledge goes completely across the riverbed and often indicates an increase in gradient. Ledges have breaks in them that frequently result in narrow, deep, fast chutes of water flowing through. Chutes can often be exhilarating to run.

Waves

At the base of a chute or other accelerated flow of current you can usually find a series of standing waves. These waves are a result of the deceleration of fast-moving water as it flows into deeper, slower water. Standing waves are scalloped in shape and uniformly spaced in a series. As long as the waves are not so large as to risk swamping your canoe, they are a delight to run. A dark smooth tongue of water followed by a series of standing waves is a sure sign to the river paddler of a clear unobstructed channel (Figs. 5–4A, 5–4B).

RIVER OBSTACLES

In addition to the general river features discussed above, there are several types of smaller or more

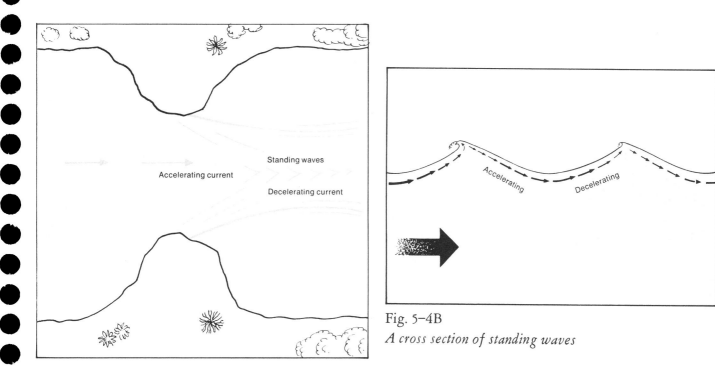

Fig. 5–4A
Standing waves at the bottom of a chute

Fig. 5–4B
A cross section of standing waves

Standing waves

Accelerating current

Decelerating current

Accelerating

Decelerating

isolated obstructions and their associated effects. These obstacles may be either visible or under water.

Underwater Obstacles

An underwater obstacle may be a rock, a log, or man-made debris, but regardless of what it is, as it lies under the current it creates turbulence that may or may not be hazardous. The type of turbulence created indicates to the experienced paddler whether or not the obstacle is a hazard. Either the rock itself or the resulting turbulence may be the hazard.

Pillows

A rock just under the surface in moving water makes its own unique mark on the surface, called a pillow. The water flowing over and around the rock appears to create a "hump," or "pillow," on the surface. It is actually a small rounded wave. If there is no current, there is no pillow. When the rock is just barely covered, the pillow will be directly over the rock. The farther under the surface

the rock is, the farther downstream the pillow will be. It takes an experienced eye to tell the difference between a pillow that indicates deep water and one that indicates a rock that your boat will hit (Figs. 5–5A, 5–5B, 5–5C).

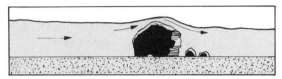

Fig. 5–5A *Surface "pillow" caused by underwater rock*

Fig. 5–5B *No current, no pillow*

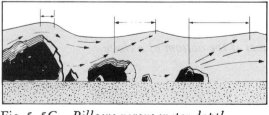

Fig. 5–5C *Pillows versus water depth*

Holes

With the more powerful currents associated with steeper gradients, an underwater rock may create what is known as a hole, or souse hole. In this case, as the water flows down the downstream side of the rock it accelerates to such a speed that it creates a depression in the surface of the water. Water from downstream then reverses and flows back to the rock and downward. There is much froth, or whitewater, associated with this condition. Small holes are not a problem if the water is deep enough to float the canoe over the rock. But larger holes may swamp a canoe, or even be so large as to hold the canoe in the hole. It is very difficult to paddle uphill (Fig. 5–6).

Sometimes holes, instead of standing waves, are created at the bottom of a chute. This will happen when the water in the chute has accelerated to a certain point and flows into relatively still water. The hazards are the same in either case. Isolated holes are easily avoided if you recognize in ad-

Fig. 5–6

A souse hole. Large souse holes should be avoided.

vance the smooth glassy water followed by a sharp line, then turbulent whitewater.

Visible Obstacles

Obstacles that extend above the surface of the water are the easiest to recognize and avoid. Most commonly these obstacles are rocks.

Cushions

Water striking a solid object will stop and then turn aside to go around it. This reaction creates a cushion of still water right next to the rock and thus helps to deflect floating objects such as your boat. Also, the water will pile up higher on the upstream side. For this reason if your boat hits a rock broadside and sticks, you will need to immediately lean downstream, onto the rock, to let the upstream side lift with the climbing water. Otherwise, the water may climb over the side of your boat and either swamp or capsize it.

A rock in a fast current without a cushion is very likely to be undercut by the current and should be avoided at any cost.

V's

Rocks also cause what are known as upstream V's and downstream V's. These can best be described as being like the wake of a boat moving through the water. In this case, however, the rock creating the wake is stationary, while the water moves.

An *upstream V* is created with the rock at the upstream point and a wake, or turbulence, fanning out from it downstream. Its name comes from the fact that the V points upstream (Fig. 5–7). You should avoid the point of upstream V's.

A *downstream V* is the result of the intersection of two upstream V's; it indicates a clear channel between obstructions.

Eddies

The deflecting of the current by a solid obstruction will create an eddy. Earlier it was noted that an eddy is found around the inside of a bend in the riverbed. Eddies are also created in the river channel itself behind rocks or other obstacles. The deflecting of the water at an obstruction creates a low spot in the water. Water from farther downstream will flow into this low spot (Fig. 5–8).

It is important for paddlers to recognize the boundary between conflicting currents caused by eddies. These boundaries are called eddy lines and are a type of current differential. A current differential is a difference in the speed or direction, or both, of adjacent currents. The current differen-

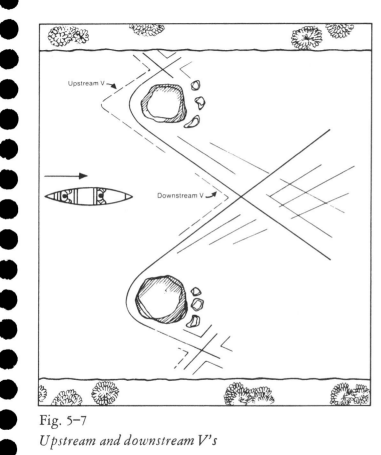

Fig. 5–7
Upstream and downstream V's

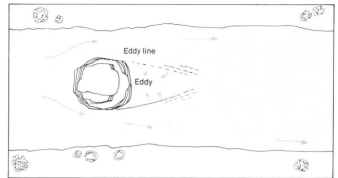

Fig. 5–8
An eddy downstream of a rock

tial is strongest at the uppermost end of an eddy. Crossing a current differential without warning or preparations may very well result in the capsizing of your boat.

Strainers

Strainers are a type of river obstruction that allow the current to flow through but catch, or "strain" out, floating objects such as boats and paddlers. Strainers are frequently located along the outside bank of a river bend because of the rapid erosion of that bank (see Fig. 5–2). For this reason, river bends should be approached with caution. Strainers may also be found elsewhere on the river, especially after periods of high water levels. You should avoid strainers at all costs because if you become caught in one, there is very little either you or others in your group can do about the situation in a strong current. You should be aware that strainers are most likely to be found on small, narrow, steep rivers as opposed to large, wide, flat rivers. Always be alert for strainers in swift water and avoid them.

Riverwide Obstacles

There are two general types of riverwide obstruction that should concern you as a paddler: manmade obstructions such as dams, and natural obstructions such as waterfalls. These obstructions pose several peculiar problems. First is the tremendous power involved in the descent of the water over the obstruction. Second, there is no route that can be paddled past it, as there is in other types of river obstructions. Last, the obstructions are hard for you the paddler to recognize from your boat on the river.

The powerful and turbulent water associated with these obstacles is found downstream and below the obstruction. It is, generally, out of your sight. If the telltale signs are not recognized in time, you may be too close to the edge and end up being carried over it by the accelerating current.

An indicator of a dam or a waterfall is a "horizon line," which is an area of smooth, calm-looking water followed by a line, indicating that the river drops out of sight to reappear farther downstream (Fig. 5–9). Most dams will have some type of superstructure on either bank of the river.

Low-Head Dams
Such dams may seem to be an exciting challenge to your canoeing skills, but you should avoid all dams by carrying your canoe around them. Even small dams with only a slight vertical drop can

Fig. 5–9

The horizon line indicates a waterfall, dam, or other sharp drop. Stop to scout *from shore.*

create holes and reversals that are virtually impossible to escape from without aid. It is frequently possible for logs and other debris to be trapped in such a reversal for days. Do not let yourself be caught in a similar manner. The danger of such a reversal below a dam is that it is even and uniform from bank to bank with none of the natural breaks or chutes that enable you to paddle through most natural ledges (Fig. 5-10).

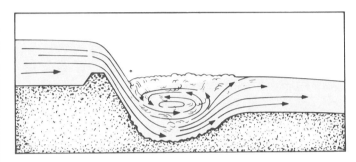

Fig. 5–10

A typical low-head dam with its dangerous souse hole

Waterfalls

These obstructions are in the same general category as dams but may typically involve larger vertical drops. The same rule of thumb applies. Know if they exist on your proposed trip and where they are located and avoid them by carrying your canoe around them. *Do not paddle over a dam or a waterfall.*

THE INTERNATIONAL SCALE OF RIVER DIFFICULTY

The various combinations of river features give a stream its character and determine its difficulty for paddling. Commonly paddled rivers and streams have been categorized under the International Scale of River Difficulty (Fig. 5–11). This scale has evolved over a period of years and is accepted and utilized by virtually all paddling organizations and river guidebooks. Not only are individual rapids classified in the scale, but an entire section of a river may be so classified.

If rapids on a river generally fit into one of the following classifications, but the water temperature is below 50 degrees Fahrenheit, or if the trip is an extended trip in a wilderness area, the river should be considered one class more difficult than normal.

Fig. 5–11
The International Scale of River Difficulty
5.14

Fig. 5–11 *The International Scale of River Difficulty*

Class I. Moving water with a few riffles and small waves. Few or no obstructions.

Class II. Easy rapids with waves up to 3 feet, and wide, clear channels that are obvious without scouting. Some maneuvering is required.

Class III. Rapids with high, irregular waves often capable of swamping an open canoe. Nar-row passages that often require complex maneuvering. May require scouting from shore.

Class IV. Long, difficult rapids with constricted passages that often require precise maneuvering in very turbulent waters. Scouting from shore is often necessary, and conditions make rescue difficult. Generally not possible for open canoes. Boaters in covered canoes and kayaks should be able to Eskimo roll.

Class V. Extremely difficult, long, and very violent rapids with highly congested routes which nearly always must be scouted from shore. Rescue conditions are difficult and there is significant hazard to life in event of a mishap. Ability to Eskimo roll is essential for kayaks and canoes.

Class VI. Difficulties of Class V carried to the extreme of navigability. Nearly impossible and very dangerous. For teams of experts only, after close study and with all precautions taken.*

---

*Reprinted from the Safety Code of the American Whitewater Affiliation, by permission.

RIVER SAFETY

When you venture onto rivers it is essential that you be aware of the potential hazards associated with this activity. You must realize that not only will you get wet, but sometimes you will even be plunged into swift water, and you should therefore dress so that you will stay warm even if you are soaked and the air and water are cold. You cannot dress properly unless you know what to expect of both the air and the water temperature. Nearly everyone who frequently ventures onto rivers has invested in some wetsuit articles, such as socks, a vest, and shorts.

As pointed out previously, you should always wear your life jacket because that enables you to perform the tasks that are needed for carrying out your own rescue. Without a life jacket you would not be able to float high enough to see where you are or to do anything but survive— if you are lucky. No one belongs on a river unless he is wearing a properly fitted life jacket.

One important element in river safety is planning your trip so that the difficulty of the river does not exceed your capabilities or that of your equipment. Every trip on the river should adhere to the safety procedures described in *Whitewater in an Open Canoe* (ARC 2173). Every stream guidebook provides information about the difficulty of streams under optimal paddling conditions. You must keep in mind that temperature and water level greatly affect the difficulty of rapids. Any river or stream at flood level should be avoided. High water can be recognized by the fact that the water is fast, dirty, and flowing through the surrounding trees or shrubbery. Refer to the section on trip planning in Chapter 2.

Once your trip has started and you are on the river, safety is very much a matter of recognizing hazards in advance and avoiding them. These hazards include souse holes, rocks, steep drops, dams, falls, and strainers. By far the most common situation from which you will need to extricate yourself is a swim that results from capsizing or swamping.

Swimming a Rapid

Whenever you are paddling on a river, if you should find yourself in the water you should immediately get to the upstream side or end of the boat and hang on to it. Always keep your feet at the surface and look downstream, as best you can, for a likely eddy (Fig. 5–12). Strong kicks and arm strokes are required to get yourself and your boat in the eddy. (This maneuver should be practiced in reasonably safe currents with rescue personnel close at hand.)

Hold on to your boat. The exceptions to this rule are rare. If your boat is properly downstream of you, it is your biggest and best life preserver, even though you are wearing a life jacket. You will not submerge as easily, you will be easier to spot, and you will be a bigger target for a thrown rope.

Look for a rope. At difficult rapids, a member of the group would be stationed with a throw rope, as described on page 3.52 . If you receive a thrown rope, snub it at the extreme upstream end

Fig. 5–12
Swimming a rapid. Keep feet at the surface and pointed downstream. Stay on your back and upstream of the boat.

of your boat (on a grab loop or thwart), *never tie it*. Hold on to the doubled rope so that you can let it slip if the rescue attempt goes amiss. If you are unable to hold the boat, let it go and permit the rope to swing you to shore. If for any reason staying with the boat endangers you, leave it and head for the safety of shore. Extremely cold water is an example of a situation that makes it advisable to abandon your boat and proceed immediately to shore.

Should you become separated from or abandon your boat, get on your back and get your feet up. Look for an eddy downstream and make your way toward it, staying on your back. Watch for strainers and snags and avoid them. Also keep an eye out for a rope being thrown to you and be careful not to get tangled in a rope in fast water. *Never tie or wrap the rope around any part of your body.* Just hang on to it.

Caution: Never attempt to stand up in fast currents. Your foot or leg could become trapped.

Once you are trapped, the force of the water on your body will hold you helpless under the surface. Avoid this possibility by keeping your feet up and downstream of you while you stay on your back.

Put your feet down only in an eddy or a slow current or if the water is too shallow for swimming.

Rescue of Trapped Equipment

Occasionally, equipment becomes trapped against obstructions. This situation presents problems that are extremely difficult if not impossible for the novice paddler to solve. Added flotation gear in the boat can reduce this risk. Successful rescue of equipment in such circumstances requires a complete understanding of the forces at work and a practiced hand at solving the problem.

The removal of a boat pinned on a rock is not an easy task. Open canoes are especially difficult to salvage. The problem is compounded if the bottom of the canoe is against the rock and the interior of the boat is thereby flooded. Once pinned, a canoe undergoes stresses and forces that are almost beyond belief. The quicker a rescue is begun, the less chance there is for serious damage to occur. Also, the easier the craft will be to remove.

If you are a novice paddler, you should travel rivers with more experienced boaters. If a boat should become pinned, offer your assistance and do only as you are told by the person in charge. Many hands are required to salvage pinned boats. In this way you will learn not only how to rescue pinned boats but how to be of the greatest possible benefit to the rescue team.

Entrapment

It is a tragic situation when a boater becomes pinned in a strainer or is the victim of a foot trapping. Fatalities are often the result. The victim, once pinned or trapped, is in a fast current that forces the torso and head beneath the surface of the water. The force holding him there is so great that he cannot overcome it and he drowns.

If the victim's head is above water, the rescuers have more time to set up. Often, though, the victim must struggle against the current to maintain this position. In that case, his position must be stabilized. Once that has been done, additional effort can be directed toward freeing him. Do not be complacent—the situation can deteriorate rapidly, putting the victim in a worse, perhaps fatal, position.

Creating an artificial obstruction immediately upstream of the victim can be tried if the water is shallow or the current is not too swift. The resulting eddy can give enough slack in the force of the current against the victim so that you can remove him from the obstruction or strainer. This practice, however, is at best hazardous to the rescuers as well as to the victim and is futile in deep or fast-moving water.

Do not give up easily; cold water lowers metabolism, and this lowered metabolism, combined with reasonably good physical condition of the victim, could permit him to survive much longer than you might expect. Mouth-to-mouth resuscitation or cardiopulmonary resuscitation (CPR) should be given at once to an unconscious victim who is not breathing.

Do not forget to send someone for medical or

emergency assistance if that is needed. This should be done immediately. Every trip leader should be well informed about locally available emergency services.

The Throw Rope

All organized groups will set up a throw rope or two below any difficult rapid before they run that rapid. Every paddler should understand how to use a throw rope, and on the river every boat should have one. The use of a throw rope bag is described in Chapter 3. The location of the throw rope in reference to the rapid is of great importance. The rope must be stationed far enough downstream of the rapid so that once a capsizing occurs, the paddlers will have recovered back to the surface and be looking for assistance. The rope will also need to be upstream of any other turbulent water, so that the rope will not let the paddlers drift into further trouble.

If you are going to throw the rope out to the paddlers, make sure that you have their attention.

Yell "Rope!" and make sure that they are looking at you. It is desirable to have two or more ropes stationed on the river, especially with tandem canoes. Also, in swift current you will have only one try before the paddlers may be swept out of range (Fig. 5–13).

As soon as you throw the rope, you should belay it. When the swimmer takes hold of the rope and the current takes up the slack, there may be a tremendous pull. The rope, or you and the rope, may be dragged into the river unless you are prepared for it with a good belay.

AWA River Signals

A standardized set of signals has been established jointly by the American Whitewater Affiliation and the American Canoe Association (Fig. 5–14). All river paddlers are encouraged to know and use these simple signals:

- Help
- Stop
- All Clear
- Direction (right or left)
- Attention

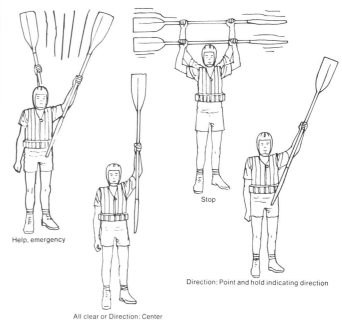

Fig. 5–13
The X marks a suitable position for a throw rope station.

The first signal is primarily three loud blasts on a whistle. It may also be given visually, as illustrated, but both should be used if possible. The next three are visual signals, done with arms or paddles, as illustrated. The Attention signal is an audible series of short whistle "chirps." Everyone on the river should have a whistle readily accessible *for emergency use only.*

When any of the signals is used, it should be passed on to the others in the group immediately.

Help, emergency

All clear or Direction: Center

Stop

Direction: Point and hold indicating direction

Fig. 5–14
American Whitewater Affiliation River Signals

Chapter 6
Basic River Canoeing

After you have developed the basic canoeing skills and they have become second nature, you and your partner are ready to prepare for river canoeing. Preparedness comes from having the proper equipment, skills, and knowledge, tempered with an awareness and appreciation of the potential hazards. This chapter presents the skills and knowledge necessary for safe, enjoyable canoeing on mild streams and rivers, including easy whitewater. Such water consists of open streams and rivers, with gentle and separated rapids—rivers of Class I or II difficulty.

EQUIPMENT

The Canoe

For river canoeing you should have a canoe that is both maneuverable and durable. Your canoe should either be keelless or have a shoe keel. Also, for maneuverability it should have some "rocker," or curvature of the bottom from bow to stern. Despite the best care and caution, all equipment is subject to very hard use on the river, especially by the beginner. Aluminum and many types of plastics have proven their durability over the years and are suitable for river use.

Other Gear

In addition to the items you should always carry (such as a first aid kit, knee pads, bailers, a throw rope and end lines), you should also have the items described below.

Waterproof Containers

These are needed for your extra clothes, first aid kit, repair kit (duct tape), and lunch. Keep in mind the likelihood of capsizing or swamping, or at least of shipping some water. Several types of common waterproof containers are shown (see Chapter 3, Fig. 3–3).

Thigh Straps

These should be a part of your canoe if you expect to do repeated river canoeing. They improve the security of your position within the canoe and afford you the opportunity for more control and stability (Fig. 6–1).

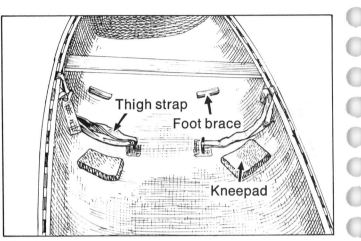

Fig. 6–1

Thigh straps and foot braces keep you firmly positioned in your canoe.

The Paddle

In river paddling your paddle must be highly durable. Wooden paddles are seldom used on the river these days except in racing. Every canoe should carry one spare paddle. It should be secured in the canoe with light string or shock cord.

Life Jackets

As always, you will need your life jacket. It should pad your back and lower spine and be comfortable enough to wear all day while you are paddling. Also, when you are in the water, your life jacket must be fully submerged to offer the greatest buoyant lift. Therefore, it must not ride up on you.

CLOTHING

Extra care is needed in selecting clothing that will keep you warm on or in the water. One thing is certain in river canoeing: you will get wet. You should expect to swamp or capsize. To be prepared, you should dress in layers and wear some wool or wetsuit garments. Shoes, shorts, and a shirt would be the minimum, followed by a sweater and long trousers, and covered with a paddling suit in colder conditions (see Chapter 4, Fig. 4–1).

Paddling Suits

These suits consist of a lightweight, waterproof nylon shell jacket and pants and are very effective in reducing heat loss from evaporation and wind chill. Closures around the waist, cuffs, and collar are either elastic or adjustable so as to best retain body warmth.

Wetsuits

River canoeists often invest in wetsuit articles to wear on the river. A wetsuit is a necessity when air or water temperatures are at or below 50 degrees Fahrenheit. A wetsuit usually consists of, at least, socks, shorts, and a vest. In colder conditions, gloves and a set of full pants and long-sleeved jacket would be needed.

Footwear

A pair of rubber-soled sneakers is usually adequate. Some people like plastic sandals. Only on a wilderness trip would heavier boots be needed, and even then not for paddling but for portages. Remember, you will need shoes that are adequate for hiking to safety in an emergency.

RIVER READING REVIEW

Once you are sure of the adequacy of your equipment, start reviewing your knowledge of the river (see Chaper 5): currents, eddies, holes, pillows, standing waves, chutes, upstream and downstream V's, strainers, and horizon lines. You will need to recognize all these features from your canoe, in advance, as you approach them from upstream. The place to begin identifying these features is from shore. As a beginner you will make a few mistakes and leave your mark on a few rocks in the river. It takes practice and experience to be able to "read the river" and select a clear course through a rapid. Often it is necessary to change your route as you progress into and through the rapid. The ability to read the river quickly is therefore vital. You must be familiar with all the river features discussed in Chapter 5, before you venture onto the river.

RIVER SAFETY REVIEW

In addition to your knowledge of the river, there are some basic procedures for safety and rescue that you must know. Your first line of defense is to be properly equipped. *One rule of thumb is to be prepared to swim any rapid you attempt to paddle.* Second, you must know what to do when you end up in the water. *Never attempt to stand in swift water.* Keep your feet at the surface and downstream of you as you float on your back (see Chapter 5, Fig. 5–12). This maneuver will allow you to fend off rocks with your feet and avoid foot or leg entrapment. Work your way to shore, if necessary by swimming directly across the current to reach shore or an eddy. Let your life jacket do the work of keeping you afloat. You should practice this maneuver in a gentle current under the supervision of your instructor. Also, try it as you hang on to the upstream end of your swamped canoe (using the end line). Never let yourself get caught downstream of a swamped canoe. If you ever find yourself in this position, do everything possible to get away from the canoe. Know and abide by the safety procedures described in *Whitewater in an Open Canoe* (ARC 2173).

THE RIVER SITE

After you have gathered and checked all your equipment, and your instructor has located an ideal spot on the river, it is time to start your skills practice. An ideal location will have a large area of calm water from shore to shore. Upstream there should be a distinct eddy along each shore, one upstream of the other. The main current in midstream between the eddies should have a speed about equal to your maximum forward paddling speed. There should be no obstruction to cause problems. The calm pool should be sufficiently large for you to recover from an upset without being carried into rapids downstream. Such a location will provide an opportunity to practice under supervision, in one safe place, nearly all of the river maneuvers you need to know (Fig. 6–2).

Once you have located this spot and once you understand how to "read" a river, your instructor will have you warm up by practicing a few basic maneuvers in the calm water of the eddy. You should practice a few pivot turns,

sideslips, and straight lines (forward and backward). Also, try a few turns with the Duffek. Refer to the paddling drills in Chapter 3.

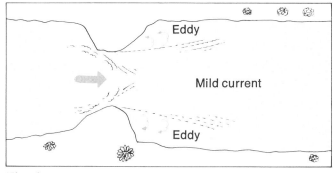

Fig. 6–2

An ideal site to begin practicing river skills

SUPPLEMENTARY RIVER STROKES

The high brace, the low brace, and the compound backstroke are necessary on the river and are described below.

The High Brace

Purpose. To maintain, or regain, a stable position.

Description. The blade enters the water a comfortable distance out to the side of the paddler, as in the draw. The blade is parallel to the keel line. The lower arm is extended at the same time as the top arm is extended and cocked with its hand near the head. The paddle is diagonal to the water surface.

Power is applied to the power face with the lower arm pulling down and toward the side of the canoe, perpendicular to the keel line. The top arm pushes up and out from in front of the body. The hips, and especially the knee on the paddling side, sharply pull the canoe into a level position directly underneath the paddler.

The stroke ends as the canoe and paddler regain stability. The blade does not usually move more than 1 or 2 feet. To recover, the blade is sliced through the water to the next stroke or is lifted from the water and swung, feathered, in an arc to the next stroke.

Synopsis. The canoe will sharply regain a stabilized trim and move slightly sideways toward the paddle side. The paddler should be able to place a good deal of his body weight onto the high brace and recover to a stable position. In moving water the paddler should use a climbing angle to add power to the brace (Fig. 6–3).

Fig. 6–3
The high brace

The Low Brace

Purpose. To powerfully return the canoe and paddler to a stable position.

Description. The entire paddle is extended out to the side of the paddler, with the grip in the water and the paddle flat on the surface. The shoulders are rotated to the paddle side, and the upper torso is extended out over the paddle. The lower arm is bent, with its elbow over the shaft. The back face is facing downward.

The lower arm and entire upper torso sharply push down on the back face as the hips and knees pull the canoe back into a stable position under the paddler. The knee on the paddling side should pull sharply upward as the other knee pushes downward on the bottom of the canoe.

The stroke ends as the canoe regains stability, with the paddler's body bent low and forward. To recover, the blade is sliced from the water and swung, feathered, in an arc to begin another stroke.

Synopsis. A sharp flip upward of the canoe on the paddling side should occur. In moving water, a climbing angle should be utilized to add power. It is also possible to stabilize the canoe in a leaned position. The paddler should be able to place a good deal of his weight onto the low brace and recover to a stable position (Fig. 6–4).

The Compound Backstroke

Purpose. To propel the canoe straight backward with power and control.

Description. Rotate the upper body to the paddle side and farther, toward the stern. The blade enters the water alongside the stern, perpendicular to the keel line. The top arm is cocked above the head as the lower arm is bent but extended toward the stern.

Power is applied to the power face with the top arm punching and the lower arm pulling the paddle along the side of the canoe parallel to the keel line. As the paddle comes alongside the paddler, it is rotated 180 degrees to push with the back face of the blade toward the bow, parallel to the keel line,

Fig. 6–4
The low brace

as in the backstroke. Near the end of the stroke, the paddle is rotated, back face outward, and a short pry is used.

The stroke ends a comfortable distance in front of the paddler as the blade is lifted out of the water and swung, feathered, in an arc to begin another stroke.

Synopsis. The canoe will move smartly backward, without turning. The blade angle is frequently varied throughout the stroke to aid in steering by adding a drawing effect at the stern and more prying at the bow (Fig. 6–5).

Fig. 6–5
The compound backstroke

Paddling Drills

A high brace is most often used to stabilize your boat in a lean in conjunction with a turn. Try a few 90-degree turns with the draw (high brace) in the bow. Gradually shift more and more body weight onto the stroke. This is the Duffek, with emphasis on the brace.

Another drill is for your partner to rock the canoe as you try to stabilize it with your brace. Either the high or the low brace can be used. If your canoe has thigh straps, you and your partner can become quite vigorous in this drill.

The compound backstroke is most useful when you are stopping and reversing direction. You and your partner simply paddle forward, then, on signal, stop and back up the canoe. Repeat this maneuver over and over. You should be able to do this stroke without the canoe's turning or moving sideways. For best results, try this stroke along a dock or buoyed rope, as a reference. It takes close coordination and skill to do this stroke alongside an object and not hit it.

RIVER MANEUVERS

On the river it is very important for you and your partner to use the current to your advantage whenever possible. To give you a better understanding of how much difference that can make, you should try this simple exercise: Anchor a buoy along the eddy line, then slowly paddle your canoe alongside the buoy, staying in the eddy and facing upstream. Then turn the canoe around, by putting the bow into the current and keeping the buoy near the center of your canoe. This turn should be very easy to do, as the current helps. Now try turning in the other direction. Let that be a lesson! Always use the current to your advantage (Fig. 6–6).

Any current differential, that is, difference in the speed of adjacent currents, can be used to your advantage in this manner.

Ferries

If your canoe were in the middle of the river, held in place by the bow's being attached to a rope across the river, you could make it go across the

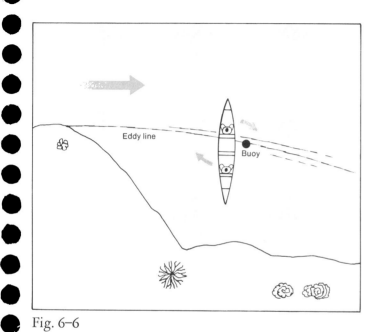

Fig. 6–6
Pivoting on an eddy line

river simply by steering the canoe at an angle to the current. If you pointed the bow to the left, the canoe would go left. The rope prevents the canoe from being swept downstream by the current, but

the current will push the canoe sideways when the canoe is held at an angle to the current (generally 30 to 45 degrees). This is how early ferries operated. You and your partner can do the same, by paddling against the current to replace the effect of the rope.

The Forward Ferry

In the forward ferry, the canoe faces upstream as you paddle forward. The bow paddler provides power as the stern paddler adds power and controls the angle of the boat to the current with draws, sweeps, or pry strokes.

The angle to the current depends on the speed of the water. Generally, the faster the water, the less the angle to the current; the slower the current, the greater the angle (Fig. 6–7).

Crossing eddy lines with strong current differentials can present problems because of the tendency of the current to tip the canoe over, as well as to turn the canoe around end for end. It is imperative that you anticipate both of these tendencies and

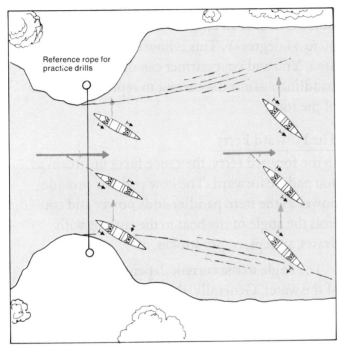

Reference rope for practice drills

Fig. 6-7

The forward ferry: a small angle in fast current, and a larger angle in slower current (generally 30 to 45 degrees respectively)

take action to counteract them. The first action you take is to lean the canoe in the direction of movement. (If you are going to your right, lean the canoe to your right.) The boat must be leaned downstream as you cross an eddy line, and it is a good idea to maintain a downstream lean at all times in a ferry (Fig. 6–8). A slight upstream lean could result in a quick capsizing.

Second, to prevent the canoe from turning around, the stern paddler must draw or pry his end of the canoe out into the current at the same time that the bow crosses the eddy line. Crossing an eddy line with speed gives the current less time to turn your canoe. It will take some practice to properly anticipate the effect of the current. Once your canoe is fully in the current, the angle is easy to maintain, as the stern paddler is the one responsible for the steering.

The Back Ferry

In many common situations on the river, the back ferry is more useful than the forward ferry because with the latter you must first turn around to face

6.12

Fig. 6–8

Lean downstream at all times during a ferry.

you in line with your chosen route and not ferry you into obstructions.

The only difference between the back ferry and the forward ferry is that in the back ferry the canoe is headed downstream and paddled backward, against the current (Fig. 6–9). The bow paddler is now in the best position to control the angle to the current, as he occupies the downstream end of the boat. The stern paddler can help, but because of the trim of the craft, the bow can steer more effectively. The bow can use the compound backstroke or diagonal draws to aid in steering.

Because the stern paddler has the best view of the angle of the canoe relative to the current, he will often give directions to the bow paddler. Since excellent communications are required to do this effectively, you should practice the back ferry until you and your partner work smoothly together. Only simple commands such as "Right" or "Left" should be used.

The same precautions are needed in crossing eddy lines or other current differentials as in the upstream. Also, in large standing waves, it is best to back-paddle to prevent shipping water. As you back-paddle, the angle must be controlled to keep

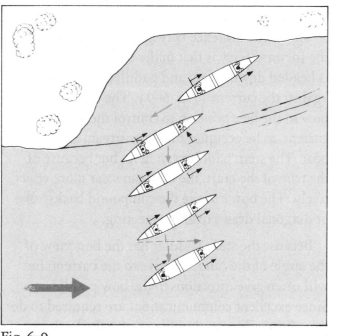

Fig. 6–9
The back ferry

forward ferry. Lean the canoe in the direction of movement downstream and anticipate that the current will try to turn you around.

In addition to ferrying from one side of the river to another, it is often necessary to back-ferry around an obstruction as you are descending a rapid (Fig. 6–10). This maneuver involves back-paddling to stop the downstream movement of the canoe, and then setting the angle to ferry to one side or the other. In this case there is no eddy line to cross. This technique is very useful and common on the river.

It is important to realize that the back ferry is essential where there is limited room to maneuver or where waves are large. This ferry also provides more time for you to react to the situation. The forward ferry, however, is easier to control and puts you into the more powerful position of paddling forward. It is an excellent adjunct to scouting from eddies.

Practice drills. As with any of your river techniques, you should first practice in gentle currents with nominal current differentials and then try progressively more powerful currents to further refine your skills. To find out if you and your partner are

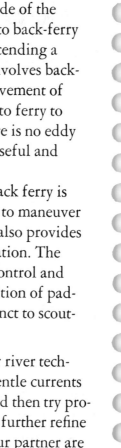

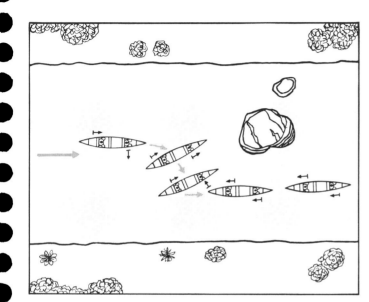

Fig. 6–10
Back-ferrying around an obstruction

really ferrying your canoe straight across the current, stretch a rope across the river where you are ferrying. The rope when in place should be well above your heads, so that there is no danger that anyone will hit it as they paddle on the river.

Start your ferry on one side of the river directly under the rope and ferry across keeping yourself under the rope all the way across (see Fig. 6–7). If you can do this in a strong current you are to be congratulated.

An exciting way to practice ferries (forward or back) is to do them across the upstream face of a standing wave. This situation will result in a surfing effect as gravity pulls your canoe down the upstream side of the wave. In this case the water, not the wave, is moving (Fig. 6–11).

Fig. 6–11
Surfing a wave. Waves can also be used to assist in ferrying.

On a properly shaped wave you will be able to surf the wave, without power strokes, with only a little steering to either maintain your position on the wave or ferry across and off it. Surfing across a wave in this manner can be an exhilarating experience.

Entering and Leaving Eddies

The eddy turn and its counterpart the peel-out are basic river maneuvers for crossing the current differential at an eddy line. As has been noted previously, a current differential is simply a difference in the speed or direction of adjacent currents. You used it earlier to turn your canoe around. An eddy line is the boundary between the main current and an eddy current. Whenever a boat crosses an eddy line two things tend to happen to the boat. First, it tends to turn around because each end of the boat is in a current moving in a different direction. River paddlers use this situation to their advantage to turn the boat around 180 degrees. Second, the canoe tends to tip over,

as would a car in a sharp, fast turn. River paddlers counteract this tendency by leaning their canoe into the turn, as a bicyclist does, and using bracing strokes to prevent leaning too far.

The Peel-out

For this example, as in the illustration (Fig. 6–12), the bow paddler is on the right and the canoe is turning to the right. You will need to start low in the eddy to get up some speed before crossing the eddy line. You should cross the eddy line at its uppermost end at an angle of about 30 to 45 degrees. As the bow crosses the eddy line, lean the canoe to the right (into the turn); the bow paddler uses the Duffek planted deep into the downstream current, and the stern paddler does a forward sweep (Fig. 6–13). The stabilizing factor is the high brace of the Duffek. It also acts as a draw to help the turn. The forward sweep in the stern helps to maintain the lean until after the boat is fully in the downstream current and moving with it.

Timing is of the utmost importance. You should

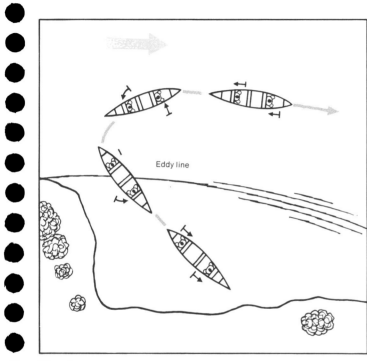

Eddy line

Fig. 6–12
The peel-out

Fig. 6–13
A peel-out to the right. The bow paddler uses the Duffek stroke, the stern paddler, a forward sweep. Lean the canoe into the turn.

start the boat lean in anticipation of crossing the eddy line. Your strokes (Duffek and forward sweep) should coincide with the entrance of the bow into the downstream current. The boat lean is needed to prevent the current from making you capsize. It is just like leaning a bicycle into a turn.

To make a broader turn, simply use more forward speed and less angle (20 to 30 degrees) when crossing the eddy line. For a sharper turn (Fig. 6–14), use less speed and a greater angle (45 to 90 degrees). Remember, the idea is to let the current, not your muscles, do the work.

To make a peel-out going to the left with the bow paddler paddling on the right, the bow would use either a pry or a cross draw, and the stern paddler would use a reverse sweep combined with a low brace (Fig. 6–15). Everything else would be the same as described above.

Practice drills. When you have mastered the peel-out in an easy current and you and your partner feel comfortable with the strokes and the boat lean, it is time to develop greater precision. Move

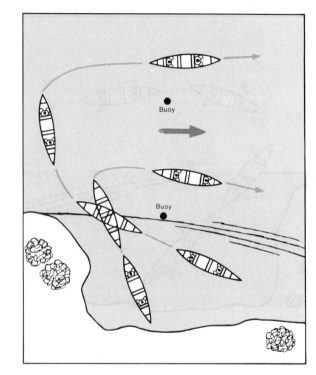

Fig. 6–14
To make a wider or narrower peel-out, change your approach speeds or vary the angle to the eddy line.

Fig. 6–15

A peel-out to the right. The bow paddler,
paddling left, uses a cross draw, the stern
paddler, a reverse sweep and low brace. Lean
the canoe into the turn.

to an area with a little stronger current. Place an anchored buoy in the main current about one canoe length out from the eddy line, about 4 or 5 feet downstream of the rock. Now try your peel-out, crossing the eddy line between the rock and the buoy and passing outside the buoy in the current. Once you can do that, try to turn more sharply and stay inside the buoy. Try this maneuver paddling on each side. That way you can practice either sharp turns or broad turns as needed. Your starting position within the eddy is an important factor.

The Eddy Turn

The eddy turn is a quick and efficient means of getting your boat into an eddy from the downstream current. This maneuver is useful for resting or scouting the river ahead. It requires close coordination between partners and good control of the boat. The eddy turn uses the current differential to turn the boat 180 degrees as it goes from the rapidly moving downstream current into the relatively calm water of the eddy. A properly executed eddy turn is shown in Figure 6–16.

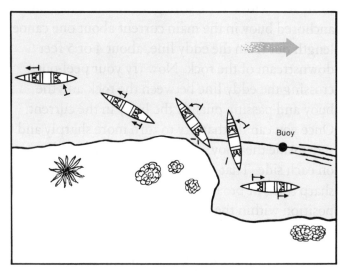

Fig. 6–16
*The eddy turn. Cross the eddy line at about
45 degrees.*

It is desirable to cross the eddy line at its farthest upstream end. Also, you must cross the eddy line with forward speed, not just drifting with the current, as the current is going downstream and not into the eddy. As the bow crosses the eddy line the canoe must be leaned into the turn, as in riding a bicycle. If the canoe is not leaned, it may capsize to the outside of the turn. At the same time the bow paddler must plant his blade deep into the eddy current with a Duffek. In this example, the bow paddler is paddling on the right and the canoe is turning to the right. The stern paddler uses a forward sweep to drive the canoe forward and turn the stern into the eddy. After the canoe is completely in the eddy, stop the turn and paddle forward to hold the canoe at the upstream end of the eddy.

You and your partner must plan the maneuver in advance because it must start well upstream of your target eddy. Approach from upstream out from the eddy so that you will be able to cross the eddy line at an angle of about 30 to 45 degrees.

To review, as you approach the eddy, both of you paddle forward to drive the canoe across the eddy line. As the bow crosses the line, lean the canoe to the right as the bow paddler plants a Duffek into the eddy and the stern paddler does a forward sweep. As the canoe turns and is completely in the eddy, the lean should be maintained until the turn is stopped; then you both paddle forward to hold the canoe into the upstream end of the eddy. Only after the canoe has stopped turning should the lean be eliminated (Fig. 6–17).

To turn into an eddy on the other side of the canoe, the bow paddler still paddles on the right, but the canoe will turn to the left. The approach is the same regardless of which side you are paddling on, out from the eddy somewhat so that the canoe can be driven across the eddy line with some speed and at an angle of about 30 to 45 degrees. As the bow crosses the eddy line, the bow paddler plants a cross-bow draw in the eddy water, and the canoe is leaned left (into the turn) as the stern paddler does a reverse sweep into a low brace, which will help the turn and stabilize the canoe (Fig. 6–18). When the canoe is completely in the eddy, you paddle forward to hold it in the upstream end of the eddy. Again, maintain the lean until after the canoe has stopped turning.

Fig. 6–17
When crossing the eddy line (turning right), lean into the turn. Here the bow paddler high-braces as the stern paddler sweeps.

6.21

CURRENT

Fig. 6–18
When crossing the eddy line (turning left) lean into the turn. Here the bow paddler cross-draws, as the stern paddler reverse-sweeps and low-braces.

In either case, a properly set up eddy turn hardly requires any strokes (but does require a lean). Once the canoe is crossing the eddy line, it will enter the eddy and turn by itself. The strokes you use are only for additional stability, speed, and efficiency. You know you have the idea of the eddy turn down pat when you can perform it with hardly any strokes. For teamwork, the command "Eddy right" or "Eddy left" is usually adequate.

Practice drills. Once you and your partner have caught on to the idea and actions necessary to execute an eddy turn, you are ready to try it in a more powerful current and with greater precision. Place an anchored buoy in the eddy about one and a half boat lengths downstream of the obstruction that is creating the eddy. The idea is to do the eddy turn without hitting the buoy, that is by doing it between the rock and the buoy. Do not forget to practice the turns both right and left and by paddling on each side.

Sideslipping

Even on calm streams, you will sometimes need to move the canoe sideways as you continue forward. This is especially true on shallow streams. It is the responsibility of the bow paddler to keep a sharp lookout for surface or underwater obstructions such as rocks, tree stumps, and ledges. Underwater obstructions are typically spotted by the bow paddler with little advance warning. The bow paddler should shout "Left" or "Right" to indicate which direction to go in, and both paddlers work together with draws, pry strokes, or cross draws to move the whole canoe sideways in that direction while maintaining their heading. You must not rely on stationary strokes, as you are not likely to be going faster than the water (Figs. 6–19A, 6–19B).

Sideslipping can be practiced on calm water, as described in Chapter 3. Keep in mind that both paddlers work together to move the boat sideways and maintain heading. The bow paddler initiates the move, and the stern paddler should respond

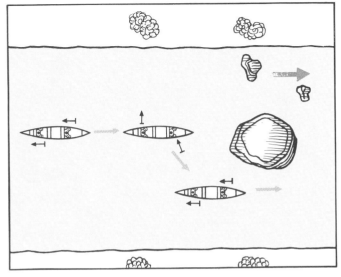

Fig. 6–19A
Sideslip around a rock on the river while staying parallel to the current.

automatically to help move the canoe in the proper direction, without turning. On the river it is important that you move the canoe directly sideways and let the current carry you past an obstruction.

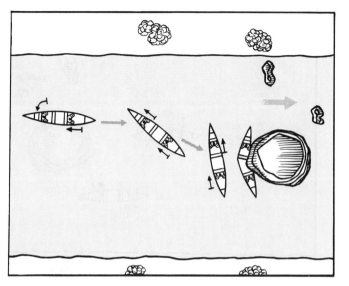

Fig. 6–19B
*Turning broadside to the current could result
in the pinning of the canoe.*

On the still waters of a lake you can turn the canoe and paddle past the obstruction, but on the river the current is always pushing you along and may pin your boat against the obstruction. On the river the surest way around a rock or other ob-struction is to sideslip or to back-ferry, which will slow or stop the downstream progress of your canoe.

Practice drills. You can practice, using a rock in a mild current, or if no rock is available, use a buoy anchored in the current. Always start practice in an easy current; then as your skills grow, use progres-sively stronger currents for your practice.

Negotiating a Rapid

Virtually every rapid you encounter as you and your friends proceed down the river after master-ing the basic river maneuvers will be unique. You will constantly be challenged to demonstrate your abilities in reading the river—to select a safe and enjoyable route and then to actually negotiate that route. A section of a hypothetical river is illus-trated in Figure 6–20, and a possible route is de-tailed showing the various maneuvers utilized. Remember, you and your partner must plan in advance a route all the way through the rapid, not past just one obstruction at a time.

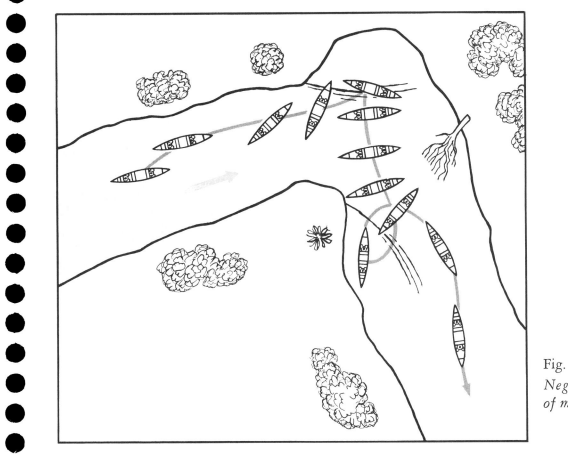

Fig. 6–20
Negotiating a rapid with a series of maneuvers

6.25

RESCUE

In addition to your having the proper equipment and the requisite skills and knowledge, it is important for you to recognize that when you are on a river, you are part of an organized group. As such, you have responsibilities to the other individuals on the trip. Everyone should be familiar with and adhere to the AWA Safety Code as presented in *Whitewater in an Open Canoe* (ARC 2173).

Part of your responsibilities includes a thorough understanding of the basic self-rescue skills described in this text. With such an understanding, in case of an upset or other difficulty, you will be less of a burden to the others. You should also be capable of lending assistance to others in need.

Almost all the basic forms of rescue can be modified under some circumstances and applied on the river, depending upon your experience and with careful consideration of the many variables that make so many river situations unique. Remember: *A swimmer should never try to stand in a swift current and must always stay upstream of a canoe in the river.*

Self-Rescue

Rocks

A common problem on rocky streams is to find your canoe stuck sideways against a rock in the current. You must act quickly to prevent this situation from becoming worse. When your canoe is stationary on the rock, the water rushes against it, rises up the side, and pours in or flips you over. It will do this most readily when your boat is broadside to the current, but it may also climb over the end of your canoe. As soon as your canoe sticks on a rock you must lean downstream onto the rock to keep from capsizing or swamping (Fig. 6–21). If your canoe swamps against a rock, the current will very likely fold your canoe neatly around the rock. *Remember: Lean downstream.*

To keep your canoe from swamping when it is being held against a rock, continue to lean downstream as you push your canoe forward or back-

CURRENT

Fig. 6–21

Canoe pinned against a rock by the current.
Lean downstream.

ward (whichever is easier) to get off the rock. It may be possible to get out of the canoe onto the rock, to lift the canoe off, and to re-enter it downstream of the rock. If you should happen to hit a rock and spin around in the process of getting yourself unstuck, don't worry, just paddle the rest of the rapid backward.

Swimming

Whenever your canoe capsizes or swamps, you and your partner become swimmers. The self-rescue techniques have been described in detail in Chapter 5, but remember:

- Stay upstream of the canoe.
- Hold on to the canoe.
- Keep your feet at the surface, downstream of you.
- Look for assistance from others. Did your group set up a rescue station in advance?
- Look for an eddy to swim into. Before running the rapid did you think of potential safety spots?

If you become separated from your canoe:

- Float on your back with your feet at the surface and downstream of you.
- Never try to stand in swift current.

Rescue of Others

Throw Rope

You may be part of the safety crew with a throw rope below a difficult rapid and so should be familiar with the use of the throw rope bag described in Chapters 3 and 5. Remember that once you get a rope to someone in the river, you must be prepared for a strong pull on the rope. Use a good belay.

Afloat Rescue

While you are on the river you can lend assistance from your own canoe in several ways. If there is sufficient room and time, it may be possible to do a canoe-over-canoe rescue, as described in Chapter 3. Be sure that the victims in the water stay on the upstream side of your canoe during this operation.

On large rivers, and especially in very cold water, it is a good idea to get a person out of the water as soon as possible. You and your partner can take one person on board your canoe, as described in Chapter 3, page 3.55. He should enter your canoe from the upstream side.

The simplest and most common assist would be to present your stern, or stern end line, to the person in the water and tow him out of the current to shore or an eddy. Use a forward ferry for this. You should be alert to possible obstructions or other hazards downstream. The extra weight and drag of a person in the water could easily cause your canoe to be swept downstream.

Remember that just getting a person to shore or out of the water does not complete the rescue. If the water is cold, you will need to make sure that he stays warm and dry. Watch for signs of hypothermia and be prepared to give treatment. Remember that being cold robs you of strength, coordination, and clarity of thought. The victim is likely to make more mistakes on the river later on if he is not properly clothed for the environmental conditions.

Rescue of Equipment

When a canoe capsizes there may be some loose gear floating away from the victims. Such gear may include paddles, loose duffel, and even the canoe. If others are assisting the paddlers, you may be needed to gather the equipment. Paddles and duffel can simply be plucked from the water and placed in the bottom of your canoe. Do not become too intent upon floating gear; remember to watch out for downstream hazards. Heavy duffel that cannot be lifted on board can be tied to an end line and towed to shore.

A swamped canoe presents other problems. If a canoe-over-canoe rescue is not possible, you will need to ferry the canoe to shore. If the swamped canoe continues to float downstream, it may become seriously damaged or destroyed against rocks. You can take it in tow by grabbing its end line, taking two or three turns around a thwart, and

holding the end line in your hand or by your teeth. *Do not tie the end line to your canoe.* You may need to release the towed canoe if it is causing you to be swept into hazardous waters.

If you cannot tow the canoe with a rope, your only alternative will be to push it to shore. Place your canoe downstream of the canoe you are pushing and try to ferry it ashore.

Armed with the proper equipment, a knowledge of the river, some experienced friends, some river paddling skills, and basic rescue skills, you are well on your way to enjoying one of the most exciting sports today: whitewater canoeing.

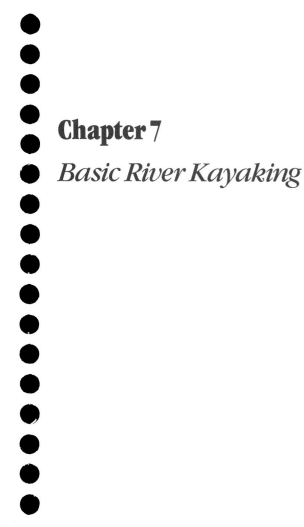

Chapter 7

Basic River Kayaking

After you have developed the basic kayaking skills and they have become second nature, you are ready to prepare for river kayaking. Preparedness comes from having the proper equipment, skills, and knowledge, tempered with an awareness and appreciation of the potential hazards. This chapter presents the skills and knowledge necessary for safe, enjoyable kayaking on mild streams and rivers, including easy whitewater. Such water consists of open streams and rivers, with gentle and separated rapids—rivers of Class I or II difficulty.

EQUIPMENT

The Kayak

The type of kayak most suitable for river use is a plastic slalom kayak. Its light weight, durability, and maneuverability make it ideal for river cruising. Although we will address ourselves primarily to the slalom kayak (as described in Chapter 4), in general the information will also apply to other types of kayaks.

For a river kayak certain features are of particular importance. It should be of flexible construction and have foam walls to support the deck. A kayak of rigid construction is more likely to be damaged in collisions with rocks. Sturdy grab loops at both ends are essential. It is also very important that the boat fit you properly. The seat, the foot braces, and the knee braces should be comfortable and hold you firmly in place. The boat is literally worn, just as clothing is.

Other Gear

Flotation Bags

Such bags are absolutely essential on the river. They should be inserted and inflated before you put the boat onto the water.

Paddles

Paddles should also be of durable material and construction. Various combinations of aluminum and plastics are popular. Your paddle should have offset, or feathered, blades and should be about 80 to 85 inches in length.

Helmets

A helmet is essential for river kayaking. It should be lightweight but should afford good protection to the temple as well as to the top and back of the head. It must, of course, be designed and constructed for use in the water.

Life Jackets

As always, your life jacket should be properly fitted and comfortable. It should not go too low on your body or it will interfere with your sitting in the cockpit. Some life jackets fold up at the bottom for comfort in a kayak.

Miscellaneous Equipment

Remember that it is always a good idea to carry a first aid kit and a repair kit, in a waterproof container. A waterproof container is also needed for a dry change of clothes, lunch, and other items you may wish to take along. You should also have a throw rope, a spray skirt, a sponge, and straps to hold on eyeglasses if you wear them.

CLOTHING

On the river, clothing is of particular concern for the kayaker. You must plan not only on getting wet but on staying wet. Clothing must be selected for its ability to retain warmth even when wet. A popular combination is a layer of wool clothing covered with a paddling suit. Such a suit consists of a jacket and pants of a light, waterproof nylon fabric. The wool or other clothing provides insulation for warmth, while the paddle suit helps shed water and reduce heat loss from wind and evaporation. Better yet is a wetsuit. Many paddlers invest in some wetsuit components: at least a vest, shorts, and socks. Shoes to protect your feet are also necessary. Sneakers or plastic sandals are popular choices. In any case, whitewater kayakers are a picturesque group (see Chapter 4, Fig. 4–1).

RIVER READING REVIEW

Once you are sure of the adequacy of your equipment, start reviewing your knowledge of the river from Chapter 5: currents, eddies, holes, pillows, standing waves, chutes, upstream and downstream V's, strainers, and horizon lines. You will need to recognize all these features from your kayak, in advance, as you approach them from upstream. The place to begin identifying them is from shore. As a beginner you will make a few mistakes and are likely to leave your mark on a few rocks in the river. It takes practice and experience to be able to "read the river" and select a clear route through a rapid. Often it is necessary to change your route as you progress into and through the rapid. The ability to read the river quickly is therefore vital. You must be familiar with all the river features discussed in Chapter 5 before you venture onto the river.

RIVER SAFETY REVIEW

Before you go out on the river you should also review the procedures for safety and rescue. *One rule of thumb is to be prepared to swim any rapid you attempt to paddle.* Second, you must know what to do when you end up in the water. *Never attempt to stand in swift water*. Keep your feet at the surface and downstream of you as you float on your back. This maneuver will allow you to fend off rocks with your feet and avoid foot or leg entrapment. Work your way to shore, if necessary by swimming directly across the current to reach shore or an eddy. Let your life jacket do the work of keeping you afloat. You should practice this maneuver in a gentle current under the supervision of your instructor. Also, try it as you hang on to the upstream end of your upset kayak (using the grab loop). Never let yourself get caught downstream of your upset kayak. If you ever find yourself in this position, do everything possible to get away from the kayak.

THE RIVER SITE

Once you are sure you have all the needed equipment, and understand how the river works and how to survive capsizing, it is time to find an appropriate spot on the river to start your skills practice. An ideal starting point will have calm water along both shores and a gently moving current in midstream. As you look upstream there will be a distinct eddy line near each shore, one upstream of the other. The current here at midstream should equal your maximum forward paddling speed. There should be no midstream obstruction. Looking downstream there will be a calm pool (Fig. 7–1). Such a location will provide the opportunity to practice nearly all the basic river maneuvers in one safe location.

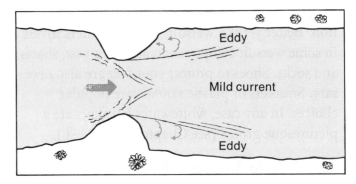

Fig. 7–1
An ideal site to begin practicing river skills

Before you venture out into the current, warm up with a few paddle drills in the calm water of an eddy. First do a few pivot turns. As you perform your pivots, gradually shift more and more of your weight onto the strokes. Pivot in the other direction as well. It is important that you perform these strokes so that they brace you, by using the blade at a climbing angle, as explained in Chapter 4.

Next, practice the high brace and the low brace. You should be able to tip the kayak 90 degrees and recover to a stable position.

Practice paddling a straight line forward and backward in the calm water, and some turns using a Duffek. Do not settle for less than a 90-degree turn on the one stroke. Also, make sure you can lean the boat well into the turn.

Once you are sure that all your skills are still functioning, it is time to try a few river maneuvers at this location before you proceed down the river.

RIVER MANEUVERS

It is very important when you are on the river to use the current to your advantage whenever possi-

ble. To give you a better understanding of how much difference that can make, try this simple exercise. Anchor a buoy along the eddy line. Then turn the kayak around by putting the bow out into the downstream current and keeping the buoy alongside the cockpit (Fig. 7–2). The turn should

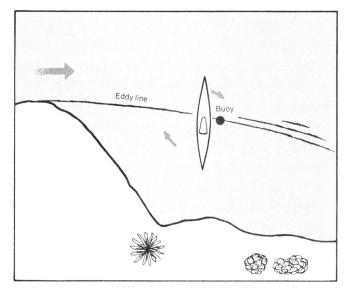

Fig. 7–2
Pivoting on an eddy line

be very easy to do, as the current is doing virtually all the work. Now try turning in the other direction. Let that be a lesson! Always use the current to your advantage. Any current differential like this can be used to your advantage in this manner.

Ferries

Early ferries on rivers were attached to a rope strung across the river and were propelled from side to side by the use of a steering oar to set the ferry at an angle to the current. The rope prevented the boat from being swept downstream as the current pushed the angled boat (30 to 45 degrees) toward shore along the rope. If the bow was turned to the left, that is the direction in which the ferry went. Modern river paddlers use the same principles but replace the action of the rope with paddling upstream against the current.

The Forward Ferry

In the forward ferry the kayak is pointed upstream and paddled forward against the current. Imagine yourself in midstream paddling straight upstream

just enough so that you are holding your position on the river. Now turn the bow to the left about 30 degrees and keep paddling while you keep the kayak at about a 30-degree angle to the current. The current will now push you toward the left. You can ferry all the way across the river in this manner without being carried downstream by the current (Fig. 7–3). You should lean the kayak downstream or in the direction of your ferry (left in this example), to avoid a possible capsizing.

A forward ferry is usually done from an eddy to some other position across the river. Crossing the eddy line presents a couple of problems. First, the current differential (adjacent currents moving in different directions or at different speeds) will tend to turn the kayak around end for end. You can prevent this from occurring by taking a strong sweep on the downstream side of the kayak just as it crosses the eddy line. If you cross the eddy line with good forward speed, there will be less time for the current to turn your kayak (Fig. 7–4).

Second, the current will try to tip your kayak

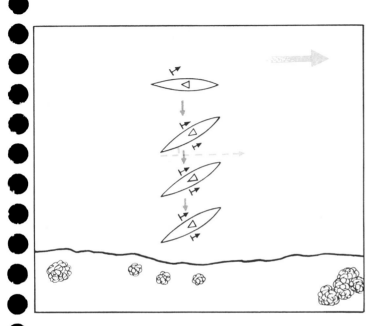

Fig. 7–3

The forward ferry from midstream to shore. Maintain a 30-to-45-degree angle to the current. Use continuous forward strokes.

Fig. 7–4

Crossing the eddy line with proper lean. A forward sweep keeps the kayak pointed upstream.

over as you cross an eddy line. To prevent this from happening, lean your kayak downstream (in the direction of your ferry) as you cross the eddy line. Once your kayak is fully in the downstream current, it will be easier to maintain control, but you should maintain a slight downstream lean.

The Back Ferry

The back ferry operates exactly the same as the forward ferry, the only difference being that your kayak is facing downstream and you are paddling backward. Start off in a mild current. Remember to cross the eddy line with some speed and at about a 30-degree angle. Anticipate the current's trying to turn you around, by using a good reverse sweep on the downstream side as your stern crosses the eddy line; do not forget to lean downstream.

Rather than back-ferrying from an eddy, it is more commonly necessary to back-ferry around an obstruction as you are descending a rapid. To accomplish this maneuver, back-paddle to stop the downstream movement of the kayak and then set the angle to ferry to one side or the other. This

maneuver is very useful and common on the river (Fig. 7–5).

Fig. 7–5
Back-ferrying around an obstruction

It is important to realize that the back ferry is essential where there is limited room to maneuver. It also provides more time for you to comprehend what is happening. The forward ferry, however, is easier to control and puts you into the more powerful position of paddling forward. It is an excellent adjunct to scouting from eddies.

Practice drills. As with any of your river techniques, you should first practice in gentle currents and then try progressively more powerful currents to further refine your skills. To find out if you are really ferrying your kayak straight across the current, you could stretch a rope across the river where you are ferrying. The rope when in place should be well above your heads, so that there is no danger that anyone will hit it as they paddle on the river. Start your ferry on one side of the river directly under the rope and ferry across keeping yourself under the rope all the way across. If you can do this in a strong current, both forward and back, you are to be congratulated.

Another exciting way to practice ferries (forward or back) is to do them across the upstream face of a standing wave. This maneuver will result in a surfing effect. In this case it is the water that is moving, not the wave (Fig. 7–6). On a properly shaped wave you will be able to surf the wave

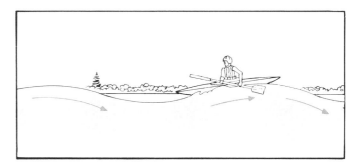

Fig. 7–6

Surfing a wave. Once on the wave, you may need only to steer.

without power strokes but with only a little steering either to maintain your position on the wave or to ferry across it and off. Surfing across a wave in this manner can be an exhilarating experience (Fig. 7–7).

Entering and Leaving Eddies

The eddy turn and its counterpart the peel-out are basic river maneuvers that use current differentials at eddy lines for turning and stopping. A

A

B

Fig. 7–7

Surfing sideways in a small souse hole. Lean downstream. Use high or low braces for stability.

current differential is simply a difference in the speed or direction of adjacent currents. Earlier you experimented with using this maneuver to turn around on an eddy line. As described in the section on the ferry, crossing an eddy line involves two effects: a tendency to tip over and a tendency to turn around. In entering and leaving eddies with the eddy turn and peel-out, you will let the current turn you around while you avoid capsizing by leaning into your turn, as you do in riding a bicycle.

You should start your practice, in the calm of an eddy, with the development of a good peel-out.

The Peel-out

You need to start in the eddy about two boat lengths from its upstream end. You want to cross the eddy line at its uppermost end with good speed and at about a 45-degree angle, as illustrated (Fig. 7–8).

As you cross the eddy line remember to lean downstream to prevent being capsized. Anticipate entering the main current. As your bow enters the main current, you should be leaning downstream and just placing your paddle in the water for a Duffek on the downstream side. Your Duffek stroke will help stabilize your lean and also help turn the kayak downstream. Once your kayak is nearly pointed downstream, you finish your Duffek by drawing toward the bow and then paddling forward. Maintain your lean until the turn is finished. Your first peel-out is complete (Fig. 7–9).

You can vary the sharpness of the peel-out by changing your speed and angle. If you paddle slowly into the eddy line, you will turn more sharply. If you use a larger angle, say 60 degrees

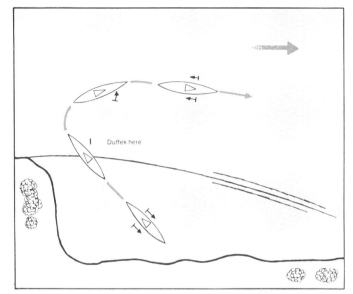

Fig. 7–8   *The peel-out. Starting with a series of forward strokes, cross the eddy line with good speed and at a 45-degree angle.*

instead of 45, you will turn more sharply still, possibly to the extent of not getting out of the eddy. Remember, the idea is to get out of the eddy and into the downstream current.

7.11

Fig. 7–9

The peel-out. Lean into the turn and use the Duffek stroke when crossing the eddy line.

Practice drills. When you have mastered the peel-out in easy currents and feel comfortable with the strokes and the boat lean, it is time to develop greater precision in the maneuver. Move to an area with a little stronger current. Place anchored buoys as illustrated in Figure 7–10. Try your peel-out in such a way that you cross the eddy line between the rock and buoy number 1 and pass outside of buoy number 2. Once you can do that, try to turn more sharply and pass between buoys number 1 and 2. This way you can practice either sharp turns or broad turns as needed. Your starting position within the eddy is an important factor. Be sure to practice peel-outs both to the left and the right.

The Eddy Turn

Getting into an eddy is very similar to the peel-out, as the basic principles of crossing an eddy line are the same as those of the peel-out. You must plan on entering the eddy from well upstream. In fact, the key to a good eddy turn is your advance positioning. In the eddy turn, the idea is to cross the eddy line at an angle of about 30 to 45 degrees at

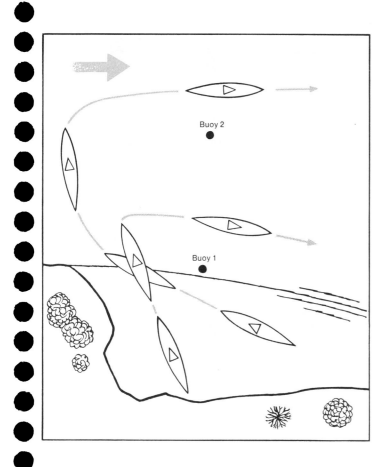

Buoy 2

Buoy 1

Fig. 7–10
To make a wider or narrower peel-out, change your approach speed and the angle to the eddy line.

its uppermost end, with good forward speed. This position will take advantage of the strongest current differential. Your kayak needs to be in the current that will pass next to the eddy and turned to cross the eddy line at an angle (Fig. 7–11). As you approach the eddy, time your forward strokes to drive the bow across the eddy line at its uppermost end. You can do this with a strong forward sweep on the left, if you turn to the right just before crossing the eddy line (Fig. 7–12). This maneuver will turn the boat and drive it forward. As the bow crosses the eddy line, plant the paddle firmly into the eddy current on your right with a Duffek. Your Duffek stroke will help stabilize your kayak and help turn you around. With stronger current differentials you will need more lean.

7.13

Fig. 7–11

The eddy turn. Driving the boat forward,
cross the eddy line at about 45 degrees.

Fig. 7–12

The eddy turn. When crossing the eddy line,
lean into the turn and use the Duffek stroke.

Practice drills. Once you have caught on to the idea and have mastered the actions necessary to execute an eddy turn, you are ready to try it in a more controlled manner. Move to an area with a slightly stronger current. Anchor a buoy as shown (see Fig. 7–11). The idea is to make the eddy turn between the rock and the buoy. Do not forget to practice eddy turns both to the right and the left.

d

e

f

Ind. 15